EAT HAPPY TOO

by

Anna Vocino

TELEMACHUS PRESS

A word of caution...

The recipes in this cookbook contain whole, real foods. It should go without saying that these recipes are in no way a "diet," but were instead borne out of a way of eating that reduces processed foods. I am not making any medical claims. I have no idea how your body functions optimally, so I'm leaving that part up to you—you are a grownup, and I assume you intend to cook recipes without sugars and grains. As with any new recipe, please read the ingredients carefully and consult your physician or dietitian before consuming if you have any sort of food allergy or medical condition.

EAT HAPPY TOO

Instant Pot® is a registered trademark of Instant Brands Inc.
Vitamix® is a registered trademark of Vitamix Corporation
NSNG® is a registered trademark of Vinnie Tortorich
Treeline® is a registered trademark of The Gardener Cheese Company, Inc.
Heidi Ho™ is a trademark of Heidi Ho Organics, LLC.
Kite Hill® is a trademark of Lyrical Foods, Inc.
Miyoko® is a trademark of Miyoko's Kitchen Corp.
Dasani® is a registered trademark of The Coca-Cola Company

Cover designed by Telemachus Press, LLC

Cover photo, back photo, and interior photos of the author by Joanna Degeneres

Food photos by Anna Vocino

Published by Telemachus Press, LLC
http://www.telemachuspress.com

Visit the author website:
http://www.annavocino.com

ISBN: 978-1-948046-78-7 (eBook)
ISBN: 978-1-945330-68-1 (Hardback)

Library of Congress Control Number:2019906640

Cookbooks / Food & Wine / Special Diet / Gluten-Free

Version 2019.10.01

Dedication

Still for Mom, who I know for sure is up there pulling harpsichord strings to make things sparkle beyond my wildest imagination.

"Only the pure of heart can make a good soup."

-Ludwig Von Beethoven

Acknowledgments

The biggest thanks goes to every single person who made the original Eat Happy a hit. I owe you all a debt of gratitude and appreciation, and this second book wouldn't even be a remote possibility if it weren't for your unwavering support. All y'all spread the word so well, and I am humbled by the great response. I can't tell you how happy I am to hear from each and every one of you that the book has done you right.

Thank you to the team at Telemachus Press: Steve and Terri Himes, the dynamic duo of publishing. Yes, you taught me all about the world of books, but you also taught me how to remain calm under pressure. You take my ideas and scant words and bring my vision to life, and you do it flawlessly and with every attention to detail I didn't even realize I was missing.

Thank you to Jackie Fogel for our brief few months getting to reconnect and work together again and for Lia Richardson who has jumped in full force to do whatever is asked of you. Thank you to Amy Collins for believing in my message and getting said message out there.

Thank you to Jeannie Hayden for not only contributing a recipe to the book, but for teaching me about Art Before Dishes so I could get a lot more done with a lot fewer excuses. Thank you to Sally Anders for contributing not just a recipe, but two wonderful daughters who have adopted me as their sister. Thank you to Tricia Clark for your recipe contribution—I wish I had you with me every day in the kitchen to class up my photo game. Thank you to Paul Cappelli and Steven Crutchfield for the bajillion wonderful things you do for me and my family, not to mention letting me swipe a family recipe for the book.

Thank you to Daniele Passantino, my beautiful friend, compass, and social media guru. Thank you for keeping me on track and for helping me grow this thing. If folks only knew how this skeleton crew of ours operates, then the world would see how much you carry on your shoulders so that Eat Happy can have a public face.

Thank you to Torri Anders for your fortitude, brains, and endurance in the kitchen. This second book would not exist except for your willingness to come to work each day and put my feet (and much food) to the fire. All while mostly fasting. I bow down to your expertise, and I constantly marvel at your support and encouragement. I miss you every day.

Thank you to Vinnie Tortorich who continues to offer endless support and encouragement. We have the best time together, and I can't thank you enough for making me start a podcast with you back in 2012. You continue to change lives and help people, and I'm humbled to be along for the journey.

Thank you to Lucy and Loren who remain ever steadfast rocks of inspiration. You both are my world and my life. And thank you to Izzy the Italian Greyhound, my most calming and constant companion, who never once ate sugars and grains, and has the body to show for it.

Foreword by Vinnie Tortorich

In 2012 I was looking for someone to help me start a podcast. I wanted to share my NSNG® weight loss secrets with the man on the street. I believed that this simple yet vital information should be available to everyone. Optimal health should be every person's right—not just the privilege of my Hollywood celebrity clientele.

A friend suggested that I contact Anna Vocino, who I had briefly met years before. She had recording equipment and a great voice. Anna graciously agreed to work with me, and my podcast Fitness Confidential was launched to much success.

Recording took place in Anna's North Hollywood studio and sometimes we were there all day. Every few hours, Anna would disappear into the house and return with mouthwatering NSNG®-friendly dishes to sustain us during these long hours. Each time it was something different, and each time it was delicious.

Anna's creations were so good that I became convinced that she should have her own cooking show. Well, in true Anna fashion, she decided not to listen to me and wrote a cookbook instead.

Eat Happy, Anna's break-out, best-selling first book, with her easy and wholesome recipes, is proof that healthy eating can be satisfying, affordable and fun.

In her second book Eat Happy, Too, Anna delves deeper into making low-carb, restaurant quality meals, offering myriad tantalizing options for substitutes that would thrill even the most fastidious of foodies. I particularly love the chapters on condiments and cocktails—areas that are always riddled with dietary booby traps.

Anna Vocino is the real deal folks—but if you have her first book Eat Happy, you already know that.

Enjoy!

Vinnie Tortorich
Author
Fitness Confidential and Creator of NSNG®

CONTENTS

WELCOME TO EAT HAPPY TOO

Welcome back to the second go around of Eat Happy. Y'all are a vocal bunch, and you made it crystal clear that the 154 recipes in the first book simply weren't enough to keep you satiated with NSNG® recipes. Well, you asked, and I answered. And I'm so glad you did. I'm thrilled to have another 160+ recipes to share with you to help augment your weekly routines and spice up your special occasions.

I'm not going to retell my story here. That's all outlined in the first book. Besides, I'm a comic at heart, and I don't like the mushy stuff. So let's get to the main event: the FOOD.

And as they relate to food, I would like to reiterate some VERY important points from the first book:

THIS IS NOT A DIET BOOK.

These are recipes made with real food. The whole philosophy behind NSNG® (No Sugars No Grains) as set forth by Vinnie Tortorich is that you eat real food until you are full, and then you stop eating because your body lets you know you are full. It's not rocket science, but if you're into that sort of thing, please read books by Gary Taubes, Nina Teicholz, and Jason Fung; and also search for Peter Attia, Gary Fettke, Ivor Cummins, Stephen Phinney, and Eric Westman on the internet. These folks (and many more) will tell you much more eloquently and scientifically why and how the body works the way it works, and why to avoid processed sugars and grains.

I'm here to give you recipes that adhere to this philosophy. If you are new to it, you're going to experience what is called a massive paradigm shift. This is not your mother's way of counting calories, macros, micros, grams or any other counting-based system of dieting...because THIS IS NOT A DIET.

I will never include nutritional information for two reasons. One, there are so many massive databases that contain nutritional information that if you insist on counting, you should use one of those sites or apps. Two, I promise you there's a pot of gold at the end of this rainbow, and when you quit eating sugars and grains long enough, you can feel your body working the way it was intended. You'll stop overeating and will no longer have the need to police yourself to stay on track. It's freedom, I promise. And it feels so good. Which brings me to my next point...

MOST OF THE DESSERTS IN THE DESSERT CHAPTER CONTAIN SOME FORM OF SUGAR.

Sugar is sugar, and sugar will cause an insulin response no matter which way you slice it. However, 100% of people who give up sugars and grains want to have a treat from time to time. That is what these dessert recipes are intended to be: a treat.

I've tested and re-tested my dessert recipes to use the least amount of sugar possible to still make the recipes work. Of course you are welcome to omit the sugar altogether or use artificial sweeteners or sugar substitutes. That is a personal choice which is up to you. I'm just giving treat options for my audience who like to have the rare indulgence. For the most part, you will be eating savory dishes, and your sweet tooth will cease to haunt you. It's liberating. But this dessert chapter is offered for those times when you need to make something for a special occasion.

Some of you come here from a baking background, and when you say you miss baking after cutting the carbs, I hear you. I have some baking recipes in both books that will hopefully satisfy these urges. I promise that eventually, you won't bake as much, and instead, you'll become obsessed with grilling that steak to the perfect doneness.

DID I MENTION THAT THIS IS NOT A DIET BOOK?

Oh, ok cool! You heard me say it! It bears repeating, and I thank you for your patience. Trust me, life is so much better when there's no counting involved. We all have more important things to get done.

A Note on Food Quality

Whenever possible, try to buy the highest quality food you have access to and can afford. I personally try to find pasture-raised meats and eggs, and organic produce. Sometimes these items are not available or sometimes they are price prohibitive. That's okay. Make the decision based on what works for you.

COOKING OILS

When cooking, I stick to using olive oil (Villa Cappelli always), coconut oil, avocado oil, butter, beef tallow, and lard. Occasionally I'll use a splash of sesame oil in a recipe. If I'm in a pinch and out of beef tallow, I'll use peanut oil for the rare occasion of deep frying when it requires a massive quantity of oil. There has been too much science on the inflammatory properties of seed oils, and we've had too many experts on the Fitness Confidential podcast tell us as much. I avoid these oils when cooking at home: canola, corn, sunflower, safflower, cottonseed, and soybean oil.

NSNG® BAKING

When folks first give up sugars and grains, they ask me these questions most frequently: "How do I make NSNG® bread?" "How do I bake NSNG® treats?" "IS there such a thing as an NSNG® cookie?" Here's the honest truth: some things work well with an NSNG® substitution, and I try to offer up recipes to fill that void. But some things DON'T. It's okay, we will all get over not figuring out how to do NSNG® puff pastry or NSNG® croissants. There are so many other things to eat. Save the splurges for when you are in Paris at the Helmut Newcake bakery (or wherever your version of this is).

There are some NSNG® items that do indeed work, like pizza crusts, stuffing, gnocchi, cauliflower tots, and more. Some of these recipes are in the first Eat Happy. These items tend to rely heavily on almond flour, coconut flour, and/or cauliflower. I try to develop recipes using a variety of these items, and not all just rely on almond flour since there are so many of you who tell me you or your kids have nut allergies.

Almond flour and coconut flour, while technically grain free, have more carbohydrates than say a steak with a side of broccoli. So if you are concerned about having an extremely high insulin resistance, you may need to back off the recipes that have a high level of baking ingredients until you have healed what's going on with you metabolically.

Arrowroot powder and xanthan gum are used in very small quantities as binders and thickeners in some recipes. If you purchase either of those products, keep them airtight in the fridge or dark pantry, and they'll last you a very long time.

Flax meal is a wonderful substitute for eggs in baking. In a small bowl, whisk together 1 tablespoon flax meal with 3 tablespoons water and let sit for a few minutes until it starts to have a jelly-like consistency. This is the equivalent of one egg. I use the flax egg quite often in recipes as I personally cycle on and off eggs.

BREAKFAST

Real eggs are the order of the day for the egg dishes in the breakfast chapter. For those days when you don't feel like fasting, or those days when you feel like brunching, there are recipes in the breakfast chapter that will satisfy those urges without having to carb out at a restaurant. I love breakfasts using leftovers from the night before. IF you're dying for pancakes, check out the Paleo Banana Pancakes. They are pan-cake-y satisfaction. Also, if you're dying for pancakes, remember, a lot of us were legit dying FROM pancakes, so remember how far you've come on this no sugar no grain journey and rejoice in the fact that you don't need to miss having "regular" pancakes anymore.

COCKTAILS

Since I get asked daily about how to make a low carb cocktail, I figured it was time to share some of my secrets. I've come up with many selections that will hopefully make you excited to play mixologist. Beer and wine are off the table—too many residual sugars/carbs. If you like to experiment, feel free to change out the distilled spirit in the recipe, and if you don't care for alcohol, you can make every recipe omitting the liquor and using more soda water. The fruits used in these recipes are muddled and puréed to retain the fiber content. But fair warning—if you're drinking several of these in a night, take it easy! If you are trying to curb fruit consumption, please stick to the trusty vodka soda with lime.

DAIRY FREE

There are lots of dairy free recipes in this cookbook. I myself am dairy free 90% of the time, so I'm quite familiar with the necessary steps to take to omit or substitute dairy. I personally prefer coconut cream (usually in a can), full fat coconut milk (in a can or box), or almond milk when a recipe requires cream or milk. Please make sure you check all labels so that you buy cream/milk with no added sugar.

For dairy free cheese, I'm a fan of the brands Treeline, Heidi Ho, Kite Hill, and Miyoko. Sometimes these brands are available in stores, sometimes they're not. I find the best tasting dairy free cheeses are made from nuts, and if you have a nut allergy, you may not be able to partake in these cheeses.

When a recipe requires a creamy base where you would ordinarily use sour cream, cream cheese, or crème fraîche, I like soaking cashews and puréeing them with zucchini. You'll find this theme recurring throughout the book with dressings and creamy garnishes. Full fat coconut cream/milk in the can also works well for this application.

Some recipes do not lend themselves to dairy free substitutes, and for that, I apologize. Make those recipes for friends or you can always rip those pages out of the book and burn them.

As always I encourage you to substitute, experiment, and play around with recipes so that you can come up with solutions that make you happy.

And speaking of experimentation...

You have my blessing! Let me know what you come up with by tagging me in your pictures on all the socials. @AnnaVocino thank you very much.

Now, let's make some food!

EAT HAPPY
TOO

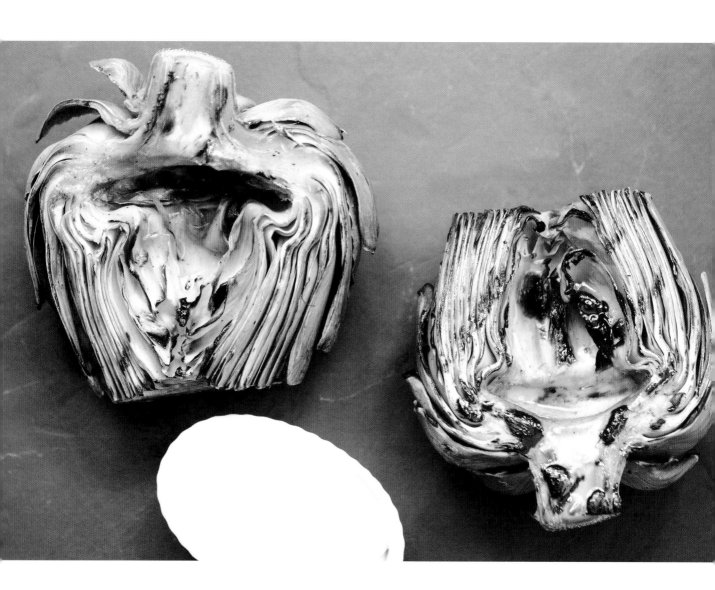

STARTERS

Jalapeño Poppers

(Yields 20 Poppers)

These Jalapeño Poppers have a spicy kick, some rich, gooey cheese, and none of the bar food high-carb trappings of the poppers you get at your local pub. These little cuties are not deep fried in gluten-y batter, but instead, topped with a coating of seasoned almond flour and baked in the oven. You won't miss the batter.

---

10 jalapeño peppers, sliced in half, deseeded and deveined
2 slices bacon, cooked, cooled, and broken into pieces
1 8-ounce package of cream cheese, softened to room temperature
1/2 cup Colby Jack shredded cheese
3/4 teaspoon garlic powder, divided
1/2 cup almond flour
1/4 teaspoon salt
1/8 teaspoon ground cayenne pepper

Preheat oven to 350°. Lay jalapeño halves on a foil-lined baking sheet. In a mixing bowl, fold in bacon pieces, cream cheese, shredded Colby Jack, and 1/2 teaspoon of garlic powder. Spoon mixture into jalapeño halves until distributed evenly. In smaller mixing bowl, whisk together topping ingredients—almond flour, ground cayenne, salt, and remaining 1/4 teaspoon garlic powder. Sprinkle evenly on top of cheese-filled jalapeño halves. Carefully place baking sheet of filled jalapeños into the oven. Cook for 20 minutes, then turn up oven heat to 400°, cook for 20 more minutes, or until jalapeños look soft and the tops are a golden brown.

Instant Pot Pork Rillettes

(Serves 6-8)

These are a delicious starter to make in advance, and you can freeze the remainder and serve as a main dish, or thaw right before your next party. I like serving a pork rillette nontraditionally topped with diced tomatoes in dried oregano, serving it with Rosemary and Thyme Chips (p. 20).

2 pound pork shoulder or butt, cut into 1" cubes
2 teaspoons salt
1/2 teaspoon pepper
1/2 teaspoon ground dried ginger
1/2 teaspoon ground nutmeg
1/2 teaspoon allspice
2 garlic cloves, peeled and halved
2 bay leaves
1/2 cup chicken broth
1 tablespoon white wine vinegar
1/2 cup olive oil
1-2 tomatoes, diced for garnish
1/2 teaspoon dried oregano, for garnish

Place pork cubes in Instant Pot. In a small mixing bowl, combine salt, pepper, ginger, nutmeg, and allspice, pour over pork cubes making sure pieces are covered. Tuck garlic clove halves and bay leaves into pork cubes. Pour over chicken broth, vinegar, and olive oil.

Close and seal Instant Pot lid and make sure Vent is set to "Sealing." Cook on "Manual" setting programmed to 30 minutes, only opening the lid after the Instant Pot has depressurized and the silver float valve has dropped completely, about 1 hour total cook time.

Remove lid, strain pork, reserving liquid. Remove and discard garlic cloves and bay leaves. Using forks or your hands, separate the pork cubes into tiny pieces. Add back in 4-6 tablespoons of reserved liquid and mix around the pork. Press pork into four small ramekins or two small mason jars. Add 1-2 more tablespoons reserved liquid to each ramekin of pork. Cover tightly with plastic wrap and keep refrigerated for up to a week. Serve hot or cold, spread on Rosemary and Thyme Chips (p. 20) or with veggies. Garnish with diced tomatoes topped with dried oregano if desired.

Smoked Salmon and Beet Salad with Lemon Herb Crème Fraîche Dressing

(Yields 4 salads)

8 ounces crème fraîche
3 teaspoons prepared horseradish, divided
Juice of one lemon
1 tablespoon fresh chives, minced
1 tablespoon fresh dill, minced
2 cups arugula
8 ounces smoked salmon, thinly sliced
1 15-ounce can of beets in water, drained and divided into 4 equal servings

In a small mixing bowl, whisk together crème fraîche, 1 teaspoon of the horseradish, lemon juice, chives, and dill into a dressing.

On one of four salad plates, spread 2 tablespoons crème fraîche dressing. Atop, arrange 1/2 cup arugula, 2 ounces smoked salmon, 1/4 of the beets on hand. Drizzle with 2 additional tablespoons of dressing. Garnish with 1/2 teaspoon of prepared horseradish. Repeat for three remaining salad plates, serve.

Torri's Hillbilly Ceviche

(Yields 5-6 cups)

Some of you might recognize Torri Anders of Torri's Chicken Legs recipe fame from Eat Happy. We are glad she's back for the sequel because without her, you wouldn't have Eat Happy Too in your hot little hands right now. Torri has moved to Phoenix, and I wish her 80% well and 20% that she would come back.

If you haven't made Torri's Chicken Legs recipe, stop what you're doing and go make them. Then come back to this ceviche, which I advise you to prepare several hours in advance of when you plan to serve it to give the flavors time to marry. Use pre-cooked shrimp, and you will save time without sacrificing flavor.

Juice of 1 orange
Juice of 3 lemons
Juice of 1 lime
1½ cups diced fresh tomatoes
1½ cups diced cucumber
1½ cups diced red bell pepper
1/2 jalapeño pepper, seeds discarded, minced
1/2 teaspoon minced garlic
2 teaspoons cilantro leaves, loosely chopped
1 teaspoon cumin
1 teaspoon salt
1/2 teaspoon freshly ground black pepper
16 ounces (1 pound) cooked, peeled, and deveined shrimp,
tails removed and discarded

In a small mixing bowl, whisk together orange, lemon, and lime juice and set aside. In a large mixing bowl, gently fold together tomatoes, cucumber, red bell pepper, jalapeño, garlic, cilantro, cumin, salt, and black pepper. Pour citrus juice over the mixture and toss. Gently fold in shrimp until all ingredients are mixed. Serve right away or chill in the refrigerator for 2-4 hours before serving to allow flavors to marry.

Steamed Mussels

(Serves 2-4)

Traditionally, steamed mussels are made with a dry white wine. I sub chicken broth and white vinegar for the wine to keep the recipe alcohol-free. Feel free to use a dry white white wine like Sauvignon Blanc or Pinot Grigio.

---

2 tablespoons olive oil
1 leek, white and palest green parts only, finely chopped
1/2 medium onion, finely chopped
Salt and pepper
1/4 cup chicken broth
1/4 cup white vinegar
2-3 pounds mussels, scrubbed clean
Lemon wedges for garnish
3 tablespoons butter, melted for dipping (optional)

In a large cast iron skillet or nonstick pan, heat olive oil to medium high heat. Sauté leeks and onions until soft, about 2-3 minutes, being careful not to burn the leeks. Season with salt and pepper. Add chicken broth and vinegar and bring boil for 30 seconds, then add mussels. Cover, reduce heat to medium low, and let steam for 5 minutes. Remove from heat and discard any mussels that didn't open. Pour mussels and liquid into serving bowl and garnish with lemon wedges and melted butter. Serve immediately.

CRAB CAKES

(Yields 8 crab cakes)

---

8 ounces jumbo lump crab meat,
pressed dry with paper towels and loosely chopped
2 tablespoons minced onion
1 tablespoon minced celery
1 tablespoon minced poblano pepper
(or you can use green or red bell pepper)
1 tablespoon Dijon mustard
1 teaspoon minced parsley
1 teaspoon salt
1/4 teaspoon pepper
3/4 cup almond flour
1 egg, beaten
2 tablespoons butter, for frying

Combine crab meat, onion, celery, bell pepper, Dijon mustard, parsley, salt, and pepper. Mix in almond flour until evenly blended. Fold in beaten egg until well mixed. Heat butter in a large cast iron pan or nonstick sauté pan on medium high heat until bubbling. Form mixture into 2" patties and place them in pan. Turn heat down to medium and fry crab cakes until golden brown and done, about 12 minutes, flipping halfway through. Remove from heat and place on paper towels to drain excess butter. Serve immediately with Remoulade Sauce.

REMOULADE SAUCE

(Yields 1 cup)

1/2 cup mayonnaise
1/2 cup sour cream
1½ teaspoons Tabasco sauce
(or your favorite sugar free hot sauce)
2 tablespoons Dijon mustard
2 tablespoons chopped chives
1 tablespoon lemon juice
1 tablespoon chopped capers
1 teaspoon minced parsley
1 teaspoon anchovy paste
1/4 teaspoon fresh ground pepper

Combine all ingredients in a small food processor. Pulse to mix, about 10-15 seconds. Serve with Crab Cakes.

CHIPPED BEEF DIP

(Yields 1½ cups)

═══════════════════════════════════

1/2 pound high quality deli roast beef, thinly sliced
4 tablespoons cream cheese, at room temperature
1/2 cup crème fraîche
Juice of half a lemon
1 teaspoon horseradish
1 teaspoon minced shallot
1 teaspoon minced fresh dill
1 teaspoon minced fresh chives, plus more for garnish
Salt and pepper

═══════════════════════════════════

Heat a large sauté pan to medium high heat and fry up roast beef slices, a few at a time, until they crisp up. Set on paper towel to cool while frying up remaining pieces. Chop the crisped roast beef slices into 1/2" pieces.

In a large mixing bowl, combine cream cheese, crème fraîche, lemon juice, horseradish, shallot, dill, and chives until well mixed. Fold in roast beef slices. Season with salt and pepper if desired. Garnish with more chopped chives and serve with Rosemary and Thyme Pita Chips (p. 20) or cut veggies.

Baba Ganouj

(Yields 1½ - 2 cups)

Making baba ganouj (eggplant dip) at home is a way to control the type of oil you consume. Most store-bought dips have nasty oils at the base of them. Canola, sunflower, safflower, cotton seed oils—no thank you. Instead, I use my favorite golden-green elixir, REAL extra virgin olive oil, which is the way Mother Nature (and every Middle Eastern grandmother) intended.

4 eggplants, peeled and sliced into 1/2 inch disks
2 tablespoons tahini
Juice of 1 lemon
1 teaspoon minced garlic
1 tablespoon Greek yogurt (optional, for creaminess)
Salt and pepper
1 tablespoon olive oil for drizzling at the finish
Chopped parsley for garnish

Preheat oven to 400°. Line a baking sheet with foil, rub surface with olive oil. Place eggplant slices on the foil-lined baking sheet. Bake in oven for 35 minutes, remove from oven and let cool.

Place roasted eggplant, tahini, lemon juice, garlic, optional Greek yogurt, salt, and pepper in a food processor and purée. Add more salt and pepper to taste if necessary. Scoop smooth baba ganouj into a dip bowl, drizzle with olive oil, and garnish with parsley.

Spinach and Mushroom Tartlets

(Yields 20-24 mini tartlets)

Tart Shell

1 tablespoon olive oil
1 cup almond flour
1/2 teaspoon onion powder
1/2 teaspoon garlic powder
1/2 teaspoon salt
1 egg white

Dredge olive oil on a paper towel and smear across the cups of a mini-muffin pan. Preheat oven to 400°. Mix all tart shell ingredients. Take one 1" ball of tart shell dough and press into mini muffin tin into a tart shell shape. If your fingers get sticky while pressing the dough, you can wet your fingers with water. Cook in oven 8-10 minutes until fully cooked through and golden brown. Remove from oven and let cool.

Tart Filling

10 ounces frozen chopped spinach
1 tablespoon olive oil
1/2 medium onion, minced
1 teaspoon minced garlic
1 8-ounce pack of baby bella mushrooms, finely chopped
Salt and pepper
1/4 cup chopped walnuts
1 tablespoon cream cheese
1/8 teaspoon nutmeg
1/4 cup parmesan cheese, plus more for garnish
2 eggs, separated

Microwave or steam frozen spinach for 6 minutes. Lay spinach on a clean kitchen towel, rolling up and pressing to remove remaining excess water. Let sit for 5-10 minutes.

Heat olive oil in a large sauté pan to medium high heat. Cook minced onion, garlic, and mushrooms about 8-10 minutes until soft. Season well with salt and pepper. Add chopped walnuts and cook for 3-4 minutes. Remove from heat, stir in cream cheese, nutmeg, and parmesan.

In a large mixing bowl, mix spinach and egg yolks. Add mushroom, onion, and garlic mixture. In a separate bowl, using a hand mixer, whisk egg whites until stiff peaks form. Gently and evenly fold egg whites into spinach and mushroom mixture. Scoop mixture into tartlet shells. Cook in oven for 7-10 minutes, remove and serve, garnished with additional freshly grated parmesan.

ROSEMARY AND THYME PITA CHIPS

(Serves 2-4)

1½ cups almond flour
1 egg
1 teaspoon olive oil plus more for drizzling
1/2 teaspoon dried or fresh thyme leaves
1/2 teaspoon dried or fresh rosemary leaves, minced
1/2 teaspoon salt, plus extra sprinkling
1/4 teaspoon pepper

Preheat oven to 350°. Whisk together almond flour, thyme, rosemary, salt, and pepper. Add egg and olive oil and mix together well, into a thick batter. Roll or press batter out evenly onto parchment paper to approximately 1/4 inch thickness. Bake for 15 minutes or until crisp and golden brown. Break apart into chips.

Rosemary Pecans

(Yields 1 cup pecans)

---

1 cup pecan pieces or halves
2 teaspoons fresh rosemary leaves, minced
1 teaspoon salt
1/4 teaspoon pepper
2 tablespoons olive oil

Preheat oven to 400°. In a large Ziplock bag, combine all ingredients and shake well to make sure pecan pieces are coated evenly with oil and spices. Pour out evenly onto a baking sheet lined with nonstick foil. Bake 4-5 minutes in oven until toasted. Remove from heat and let cool until ready to serve.

GRILL FINISHED ARTICHOKES...

(Serves 4)

2 artichokes
Juice of a whole lemon
1 teaspoon salt, plus more for seasoning
Pepper for seasoning
Olive oil, for coating

Trim top of leaves and stem off of artichokes and discard. Cut in half lengthwise. Using a spoon, scoop out the furry middle of the artichoke (the choke) and discard. In a large sauce pot or Dutch oven, boil 2 inches of water with juice of a lemon and one teaspoon of salt. Place artichoke halves into water, cut side facing up, season with salt and pepper, and cover. Let steam for 10 minutes, remove artichokes and let drain on a towel. Season with salt and brush cut side of artichokes with olive oil. Heat grill to at least 450°, grill artichokes, cut side facing down, about 3-5 minutes or until charred. Season again with salt and pepper and serve immediately with Lemon Garlic Dill Aioli.

...WITH LEMON GARLIC DILL AIOLI

(Yields 1 cup)

Two egg yolks
1/2 teaspoon salt
3 tablespoons lemon juice, divided
1/2 cup avocado oil, plus more for thinning
1/2 teaspoon minced garlic, mashed into paste
1/2 teaspoon minced fresh dill
1/4 teaspoon garlic powder
1/4 teaspoon ground turmeric
1/8 teaspoon ground cayenne

Using a hand mixer or immersion blender, mix together egg yolks, salt, and 2 tablespoons of the lemon juice. Add the oil, a tiny drizzle at a time, constantly mixing with the blender/mixer, until all the oil is blended in, and the aioli has the consistency of mayo. Add in remaining tablespoon of lemon juice, minced garlic, dill, garlic powder, turmeric, and ground cayenne and mix until well blended. If sauce is too thick, drizzle and whisk in additional oil to thin it out. Serve as a dip for Grill Finished Artichokes.

SAUSAGE STUFFED DEEP FRIED OLIVES

(Yields 2 cups deep fried olives)

1/2 pound large pitted olives (combination of black and green)
1/2 pound of your favorite uncooked sausage, discard any casing
1 egg white
1/2-1 cup almond flour
1/4 cup olive oil

Cook sausage until browned thoroughly, mincing into tiny pieces. Drain and let cool. Stuff olives with sausage. In one bowl, put egg white and in another bowl, place almond flour. Using a toothpick, dip the stuffed olive into the egg white, then press into the almond flour.

Heat up 2 tablespoons of the olive oil in a nonstick pan on medium high heat. Fry coated olives, placing them in pan in a clockwise direction, starting in the 12 o'clock position. Then flip after 3-5 minutes, about 3 turns per olive to fry all sides. Use toothpicks to help flip the olives.

Remove from heat and let cool on a paper towel to drain excess oil. Serve immediately.

Spinach and Artichoke Dip

(Yields scant 3 cups)

For this recipe, I use a can of artichoke hearts in water, drained, rough tops of stems cut off and discarded.

---

8 ounces cream cheese, brought to room temperature
8 ounces sour cream
1 tablespoon minced shallot
1 teaspoon minced garlic
2 green onions, white and palest green parts, minced
1/2 teaspoon salt
1/4 teaspoon fresh pepper
1/4 teaspoon ground cayenne pepper
1½ cups chopped fresh baby spinach leaves
1 cup chopped artichoke hearts
1/3 cup water chestnuts, chopped
1/4 teaspoon smoked paprika

In a large mixing bowl, whisk together cream cheese and sour cream. Whisk in shallot, garlic, green onions, salt, pepper, and cayenne. Fold in spinach leaves, artichoke hearts, and water chestnuts. Pour into a serving dish, garnish with smoked paprika, and serve.

Buffalo Hot Wings

(Serves 4-6)

Hot sauce is at the base of a great Buffalo wing sauce. Now, you can make your own hot sauce with cayenne peppers, vinegar, and spices, or you can use Frank's Hot Sauce, which as of printing, still has no chemicals or sugar in it. I pray that they keep it that way because these wings are easy to make and low carb for your next tailgate party or game day craving. Serve with homemade Ranch Dressing.

2-3 pounds chicken wings
Salt and pepper
Olive oil for drizzling

1/2 cup Frank's Hot Sauce
1 stick butter (8 tablespoons)
2 tablespoons white wine vinegar
1/2 teaspoon garlic powder
1/2 teaspoon salt
1/2 teaspoon smoked paprika
1/8 teaspoon ground cayenne

Preheat oven to 400°. Lay chicken wings spaced evenly on a nonstick foil-lined baking sheet. Season well with salt and pepper. Drizzle wings with olive oil. Bake in oven 30 minutes, or until cooked through.

In a large sauce pan, bring hot sauce, butter, vinegar, garlic powder, salt, smoked paprika, and cayenne to boil. Remove from heat and put into a large mixing bowl. Dredge chicken wings in sauce for 5 minutes. Place wings back onto foil-lined baking sheet (if you use the same foil, make sure you drain off the excess liquid first). Bake in oven 5-7 more minutes. Whisk Buffalo sauce then place wings back into sauce and dredge. Serve wings with homemade Ranch Dressing, celery sticks, and reserved leftover Buffalo sauce.

RANCH DRESSING

(Yields 1 cup)

---

1 cup sour cream or crème fraîche
2 tablespoons cream cheese
2 tablespoons fresh lemon juice
1 teaspoon onion powder
1 teaspoon dried dill
1 teaspoon salt
1/2 teaspoon fresh ground pepper
1/2 teaspoon garlic powder

Whisk all ingredients together and serve with Buffalo Hot Wings, or use as a dip or salad dressing.

MINI MEATBALLS

(Yields 24 mini meatballs)

1/4 cup raisins
1/2 cup cremini mushrooms, loosely chopped
1/2 cup freshly grated parmesan cheese
1 small onion, cut into chunks
1 pound of ground turkey
(or ground meat of your choosing)
1 egg
1/2 cup almond flour
2 tablespoons gluten free soy sauce
(or you can use coconut aminos)
1 teaspoon salt
1/2 teaspoon ground white pepper
Olive oil spray for baking

Preheat oven to 350°. In a food processor, pulse raisins, cremini mushrooms, parmesan, and onion chunks until a chunky paste forms.

In a large mixing bowl, add ground turkey, egg, almond flour, soy sauce, salt, white pepper, and the paste from the food processor. Mash and mix evenly with clean hands or a stiff spatula until well blended. Form into 1" balls. Lay on a nonstick foil-lined baking sheet, 1" apart. Bake in oven 30 minutes, until browned. Remove from oven, pierce each meatball with a toothpick, place on a platter, and serve immediately.

Mushroom and Walnut Pâté

(Yields 1 cup pressed pâté)

1 cup walnut pieces
1 tablespoon olive oil
2 cups chopped portobello mushrooms
1/2 small onion, chopped
1 teaspoon minced garlic
1 teaspoon salt
1 teaspoon dried minced onion
1/2 teaspoon nutritional yeast
1/2 teaspoon pepper
1 teaspoon fresh thyme leaves
1 teaspoon fresh oregano leaves or 1½ teaspoons dried oregano
2 tablespoons parsley leaves, plus more for garnish

Preheat oven to 350°. In a small nonstick sauté pan heated to medium high heat, toast walnut pieces until golden and fragrant, about 4-5 minutes, tossing frequently. Remove from heat and set aside 1 tablespoon walnut pieces for garnish.

Heat olive oil in a large nonstick sauté pan to medium high heat. Sauté mushrooms, onion, garlic, salt, dried minced onion, nutritional yeast, pepper, thyme, oregano, and parsley until cooked well, about 15 minutes. Remove from heat and let cool 10 minutes.

Place walnuts (except ones reserved for garnish) in food processor and pulse for 10 seconds. Pour in mushroom onion mixture and purée, scraping down sides every 20-30 seconds, until the pâté is puréed to your preferred level of smoothness, about 2 minutes. Pack pâté into a small bowl and refrigerate until ready to serve. Garnish with extra toasted walnuts and parsley leaves. Serve with veggie slices or Rosemary and Thyme Pita Chips (p. 20).

Pizza Dip

(Serves 8-10)

1 tablespoon olive oil
1 teaspoon minced garlic
7-10 basil leaves, chopped
1 14-ounce jar of tomatoes
2 tablespoons tomato paste
1 teaspoon salt
Fresh pepper

12 ounces cream cheese, softened to room temperature
5-6 ounces of pepperoni, chopped
3 chopped green onions
1/2 green bell pepper, chopped
1/2 cup sliced green or black olives
2 cups shredded full fat mozzarella

Preheat oven to 350°. In a large sauce pan, heat olive oil to medium high heat. Cook garlic, basil leaves, and salt until aromatic, about 2-3 minutes. Purée tomatoes and tomato paste in a blender until smooth. Pour into saucepan. Season with salt and pepper, turn heat to low and let cook 8-10 minutes. Remove from heat.

In a 9"-10" pie pan or casserole dish, spread cream cheese. Pour red sauce over cream cheese. Spread half of pepperoni into red sauce. Add green onions, bell pepper, and olives. Spread remaining half of pepperoni pieces. Top evenly with shredded mozzarella. Place on a foil-lined baking sheet in case there are any spills, and bake 30 minutes until cheese is melted and bubbly. Serve with veggies or Rosemary and Thyme Pita Chips (p. 20).

MAINS

SPAGHETTI SQUASH WITH SAUSAGE, LEEK, AND SAGE SAUCE

(Yields 2 large servings or 4 small side servings)

Can you have a dairy free pasta dish that is every bit as creamy and delicious as your dairy-eatin' friends have? YES. YOU. CAN. Make sure you use coconut cream with NO sugar added (check the label). Keep the coconut cream can in the fridge for 1-3 hours, open it, poke a hole in the top, and drain the excess water before adding the coconut cream to the dish.

For you dairy eaters, just sub 3/4 cup heavy cream for the coconut cream.

---

2 whole spaghetti squash
3 tablespoons olive oil, divided
1 leek, pale green and white parts only, chopped
12-16 ounces uncooked pork sausage with no casing
(I use Italian with no fennel seeds or traditional breakfast sausage)
2 tablespoons finely chopped sage leaves, plus more for garnish
1 14-ounce can coconut cream, water separated out and discarded
Salt and pepper

Preheat oven to 350°. Microwave spaghetti squash for 2 minutes on high. Slice squash lengthwise in half, then scrape out and discard seeds. Lay squash halves on a baking sheet face up, season with salt and pepper and drizzle with 2 tablespoons of olive oil. Put in oven and let cook for 40-45 minutes. Remove squash from oven and let cool enough to be able to use a fork to remove strands into a bowl. Season with salt and pepper.

Heat remaining tablespoon of olive oil in a large flat-bottomed sauté pan to medium high heat and add leeks. Cook 3-4 minutes until leeks are soft, being careful not to burn. Season with salt and pepper. Add in sausage and cook until browned, breaking into small pieces with a spatula. Sprinkle in sage leaves. Add coconut cream and stir in until heated and blended. Mix in spaghetti squash strands, tossing sausage mixture in evenly with spaghetti squash. Cover and let cook an additional 5-10 minutes, then serve, garnished with more chopped sage leaves.

Spaghetti Squash Carbonara

(Yields, 2 large servings or 4 small side servings)

---

2 whole spaghetti squash
Salt and pepper
4 slices thick cut bacon, cut in half lengthwise, and then into 1/2" pieces
1 tablespoon olive oil
1 teaspoon minced garlic
1 egg and 3 egg yolks
1 cup freshly grated parmesan
1 tablespoon Italian flat leaf parsley, chopped for garnish

Preheat oven to 350°. Microwave spaghetti squash for 2 minutes on high. Slice squash lengthwise in halves, then scrape out and discard seeds. Place squash halves face down on a roasting pan, and roast for 40-45 minutes, or until squash is soft. Remove from oven and use a fork to scrape the spaghetti strands out of the squash shell into a medium bowl, discard squash shells. Season spaghetti strands with salt and fresh pepper.

In a large, flat-bottomed sauté pan, heat olive oil, then fry the bacon pieces until almost cooked through. Add minced garlic and cook an additional 1-2 minutes. Add in spaghetti squash strands and toss with bacon and garlic. Season with salt and pepper.

In a medium mixing bowl, whisk together parmesan, egg, and egg yolks. When spaghetti squash mixture is nice and hot, turn off burner heat and immediately add in the parmesan egg mixture, tossing evenly. The heat from the spaghetti squash will cook the egg yolks into a smooth, creamy sauce as you mix them together. Garnish with chopped parsley and serve immediately.

Spaghetti Squash with Brussels, Chard, and Marinara

(Serves 2-3)

===

1 whole spaghetti squash
Salt and pepper
5 tablespoons olive oil, divided
1 pound Brussels sprouts, bottoms cut off and discarded, then quartered
1 pound rainbow chard or Swiss chard, cleaned well and cut into 1/2" pieces
2 teaspoons minced garlic
7-10 basil leaves, chopped, plus more for garnish
2 14-ounce cans organic diced or puréed tomatoes
1/2 6-ounce can tomato paste
Ball of fresh mozzarella, sliced (optional)

===

Preheat oven to 350°. Microwave spaghetti squash for 2 minutes on high. Slice squash lengthwise in half, then scrape out and discard seeds. Place squash halves face down on a roasting pan, and roast for 40-45 minutes, or until squash is soft. Remove from oven and use a fork to scrape the spaghetti strands out of the squash shell into a medium bowl, discard squash shells. Season spaghetti strands with salt and fresh pepper.

While roasting spaghetti squash, spread out Brussels sprouts evenly on another foil-lined baking sheet, drizzle with two tablespoons olive oil and season with salt and pepper. Roast Brussels sprouts 20-30 minutes until soft. Remove from oven.

In a large flat-bottomed sauté pan, heat remaining 3 tablespoons olive oil on medium high heat until shimmering. Cook chard until starting to wilt, about 3-4 minutes. Toss in garlic and chopped basil leaves and cook 1-2 minutes until fragrant. Add tomatoes, tomato paste, and season once again with salt and pepper. Cook 2-3 minutes, bringing to a low boil, then add in spaghetti squash, coating with tomato sauce. Let cook 4-5 minutes until spaghetti squash is soft. Add in Brussels sprouts and cook an additional 2-3 minutes. Season once more with salt and pepper. Serve immediately in bowls, garnished with a slice of fresh mozzarella and chopped basil.

Baked Cauliflower Gnocchi with Pumpkin Marinara

(Serves 2)

Pumpkin Marinara

(Yields 2 cups)

1 tablespoon olive oil
3 baby carrots, grated
1 tablespoon diced onion
1 teaspoon minced garlic
1 tablespoon chopped sage
1 tablespoon chopped basil
1 14-ounce can tomatoes, puréed
1/2 14-ounce can pumpkin purée
1/4 cup water
1/2 teaspoon cinnamon
1½ teaspoons salt
1/2 teaspoon pepper
1 teaspoon butter
2 tablespoons heavy cream

In a large sauce pan, heat olive oil to medium high heat and cook carrots, onion, garlic, sage, and basil until soft and fragrant, about 8-10 minutes. Add tomatoes and pumpkin purée, stir. Add water, cinnamon, salt, and pepper, stirring to evenly mix. Turn heat down to low, cover, and let simmer 15-20 minutes. Melt in butter and stir to mix. Stir in heavy cream. Purée sauce in a Vitamix or other strong blender. If sauce is too thick, add a tablespoon of water to thin out. Serve over Baked Cauliflower Gnocchi.

Baked Cauliflower Gnocchi

(Serves 2)

---

2 cups cauliflower "rice"
1/2 ball fresh mozzarella, excess water pressed out, then shredded (about 1 cup)
1/2 cup freshly grated parmesan
1/4 cup almond flour
1 teaspoon salt
2 egg yolks
Olive oil spray for baking sheet

Microwave cauliflower rice on high for 3-4 minutes. Remove from microwave and spread evenly between two clean kitchen towels. Press the excess water out of the cauliflower, let stand for 10 minutes, then press some more. Pour cauliflower into a medium mixing bowl. Add mozzarella, parmesan, almond flour, and salt. Using a fork, stir in egg yolks, one at a time, until mixed in. Place mixing bowl uncovered in fridge for 1 hour.

Preheat oven to 400°. Remove mixing bowl from fridge and begin forming with your hands into gnocchi—about 1" wide and 1.5" long. Place on a nonstick foil-lined baking sheet sprayed with olive oil. Bake on bottom shelf of oven for 10 minutes. Serve with Pumpkin Marinara.

PORK RIND PIZZA CRUST

(Yields one 12" pizza crust)

1½ cups mozzarella, grated
3 tablespoons cream cheese
1 egg
1 cup powdered pork rinds (pulverized in a food processor)
1/2 teaspoon dried oregano
1/2 teaspoon dried basil
1/2 teaspoon garlic powder
Your choice of sauce and pizza toppings

Preheat oven to 400°.

In a large mixing bowl, combine ingredients into a dough. Form into a ball. Drizzle olive oil onto a nonstick foil-lined baking sheet. Press the dough gently into a circle or square shape, about 1/2" thin.

Cook for 10 minutes, then remove from oven and carefully flip the crust, cook an additional 10 minutes. Remove from oven, add sauce, cheese, and your choice of pizza toppings, let cook until cheese is bubbly and melted, 5-10 more minutes.

ASIAN BEEF TACOS IN LETTUCE CUPS

(Serves 4-6)

1-2 pounds ground beef
1 tablespoon grated fresh ginger
1/4 cup minced green onions
1 teaspoon minced garlic
1 teaspoon fish sauce
1 teaspoon salt
1/2 teaspoon freshly ground pepper
1 tablespoon olive oil
1 tablespoon sesame oil
1 head butter lettuce, leaves washed and separated into individual "cups"
1/4 cup whipped cream cheese (or use Kite Hill almond cream cheese)
2 teaspoons water
1 teaspoon Sriracha
Cilantro, for garnish
Cherry tomatoes, quartered, for garnish

In a mixing bowl, combine ground beef, ginger, green onions, garlic, fish sauce, salt, and pepper until well mixed. In a cast iron pan, heat olive oil and sesame oil on medium high heat and cook beef mixture, chopping into smaller chunks, until fully browned. Strain excess oil and divide evenly among butter lettuce cups.

In a smaller bowl, whisk together cream cheese, water, and Sriracha, adding more water until you reach your desired consistency. Dollop spicy cream cheese mixture onto beef in lettuce cups and garnish with cilantro and cherry tomatoes.

STEAK AU POIVRE

(serves 4)

4 rib-eye, flat iron, petit filet, or New York strip steaks
Salt and pepper
2 tablespoons olive oil
1 tablespoon freshly ground mixed peppercorns
1 tablespoon Dijon mustard
2 tablespoons coconut cream (or use heavy cream)
2 tablespoons dry vermouth (optional)
1 tablespoon water

Season steaks liberally with salt and pepper, let stand for 15 minutes at room temperature before cooking. In a cast iron skillet on medium high heat, heat up olive oil until hot and shimmering. Cook the steaks until medium, about 2-3 minutes per side, or until desired temperature. Remove from pan and let rest on a plate.

In a mixing bowl, whisk together the freshly ground mixed peppercorns, Dijon mustard, coconut cream, dry vermouth, and water. Pour into cast iron pan and cook for a minute or two, whisking until browned. Immediately pour over steaks and serve.

Orange Beef with Broccoli

(serves 4)

===============

1 pound flat iron steak, halved and then cut into 1/8" thick pieces
3 tablespoons gluten free soy sauce, divided
(or you can use coconut aminos)
Black pepper for seasoning
2 green onions, palest white parts minced,
reserve green parts, chopped for garnish
3 teaspoons olive oil, divided
1 teaspoon grated fresh ginger
1/2 teaspoon minced garlic
1/8 teaspoon red pepper flakes
1/2 teaspoon minced orange zest
Juice of 1 orange
1 tablespoon sesame oil
1/2 cup water
3 cups broccoli florets (about 2 crowns, chopped into florets)
2 teaspoons arrowroot powder
1 tablespoon toasted sesame seeds

===============

In a medium bowl, toss beef pieces and 2 tablespoons of the soy sauce until beef is coated, then season with pepper. Let sit for 10 minutes. In a separate bowl, whisk together minced green onions, 1 teaspoon olive oil, fresh ginger, garlic, red pepper flakes, orange zest, orange juice, sesame oil, and remaining 1 tablespoon soy sauce. Set aside.

In a large nonstick sauté pan or wok, heat 1 teaspoon olive oil until shimmering. Add beef pieces to pan, discarding any excess soy sauce, and cook for 1-2 minutes per side. Remove beef to a plate.

Add remaining 1 teaspoon olive oil to pan, add water and broccoli florets, cover and let steam for 2-3 minutes until broccoli turns bright green. Remove lid, drain off excess water, move broccoli to outer edges of the pan. Pour in onion/ginger mixture, and heat for 1 minute, until fragrant. Fold in broccoli until broccoli is coated. Fold beef pieces back into pan. Sprinkle and stir in arrowroot powder. Cook until thickened, about 1-2 minutes, stirring often. Remove from heat, garnish with green parts of green onions and toasted sesame seeds.

BEEF KABOBS

(Yields 8-10 kabobs)

2/3 cup olive oil, plus more for drizzling
4 teaspoons salt, plus more for seasoning
1 teaspoon pepper, plus more for seasoning
1½ teaspoons cumin
1½ teaspoons ground cardamom
1 teaspoon onion powder
1 teaspoon garlic powder
1½ teaspoons dried harissa (or 1/2 teaspoon ground cayenne)
2-3 pound boneless London broil steak, chopped into 1½" cubes
(or you can use ribeye steak if you feel fancy)
3 bell peppers, preferably different colors
1 red onion

In a large bowl whisk together the olive oil, salt, pepper, cumin, cardamom, onion powder, garlic powder, and dried harissa. Season the cubed meat with salt and pepper and place cubes into a large Ziploc bag. Pour the marinade into the Ziploc bag, and shake the bag around to mix marinade and to make sure the beef is coated. Refrigerate beef 2-6 hours.

Cut the peppers and onion into 1½" pieces. Place in a large bowl and season with salt and pepper. Drizzle with olive oil and toss with hands to make sure all veggie pieces are coated with a little bit of oil.

Heat grill to 450-500°. If using bamboo skewers, make sure to soak them for 15 minutes before threading meat and veggies. Thread meat pieces and vegetable pieces onto skewers, leaving enough room at both ends to handle the skewer. Grill skewers 5-7 minutes on each side, until meat is done through. Serve immediately.

CARNE ASADA DRY RUB

(Serves 4-6)

2 pounds skirt steak (also called flap meat)
1 tablespoon ancho chili powder
1 tablespoon smoked paprika
1 teaspoon cumin
1 teaspoon dried oregano
1 teaspoon garlic powder
1 teaspoon salt
1/2 teaspoon allspice
1/2 teaspoon onion powder
1/2 teaspoon freshly ground pepper
1/4 teaspoon ground cayenne pepper
Lime wedges, chopped cilantro, Pico De Gallo, and chopped onions for serving

Lay skirt steak flat on a large baking sheet. In a small mixing bowl, whisk together all dry spices then rub evenly into both sides of the skirt steak. Heat a grill up to 500° and grill each side for 2-4 minutes, depending on thickness of the meat. Remove from grill, let stand 5-7 minutes, then slice into steak portions, and serve with lime wedges, chopped cilantro, Pico De Gallo (p. 225), and chopped onions.

Lime Tequila Fajitas
(Serves 4-6)

1½-2 pound flank steak
Salt and pepper, plus more salt for marinade
1/2 cup tequila
Juice of 4 limes
Juice of 2 oranges
1 teaspoon cumin
1/2 teaspoon garlic powder
1/2 teaspoon onion powder
1/2 teaspoon ground white pepper
1/4 teaspoon red pepper flakes
2 yellow, red, or orange bell peppers, sliced
2 onions, sliced
2 tablespoons olive oil
2 heirloom tomatoes, cut into wedges, for serving
Avocado slices, cheese, sour cream, salsa, hot sauce, cilantro, Pico De Gallo,
or your preferred garnish

Season flank steak well with salt and pepper. In a mixing bowl, whisk together 1 teaspoon salt, with tequila, lime juice, orange juice, cumin, garlic powder, onion powder, white pepper, and red pepper flakes. Pour marinade into a Ziploc baggie and drop flank steak into bag, sealing and shaking to coat flank steak fully with marinade. Place bag in fridge 2-3 hours.

Remove flank steak from fridge and bring meat to room temperature. Place bell pepper and onion slices in a large mixing bowl. Drizzle olive oil over slices and season well with salt and pepper. Pour onion and pepper slices onto a vegetable grill pan. Heat grill to 450-500°. Grill flank steak 7-9 minutes per side, remove from grill and let stand 5 minutes. Slice thinly on the diagonal.

Grill veggies 2-3 minutes, until soft and starting to char. Remove from grill. Serve sliced meat with grilled peppers and onions and tomato wedges. Garnish with avocado slices, cheese, sour cream, salsa, hot sauce, cilantro, or Pico De Gallo (p. 225).

MOTHER SALLY'S BEEF STROGANOFF

(Serves 4-6)

Stroganoff is traditionally laden with sour cream and slathered all over egg noodles. But thanks to the generosity of one of my favorite moms, Sally Anders, this recipe flips the script to give the dairy free people an option—minus the egg noodles. If you are a dairy-lovin' type, you can still have it your way...just substitute regular sour cream or greek yogurt for the dairy free yogurt.

1-2 pounds of beef eye-of-round roast, cut into 2" long by 1/2" wide pieces
Salt and pepper
4 tablespoons olive oil, divided
16 ounces of sliced mushrooms
1 medium to large onion, sliced
1 cup water
1 cup full fat canned coconut milk or coconut cream
2 tablespoons dairy free plain yogurt
1 teaspoon minced garlic
1 tablespoon tomato paste
1 tablespoon Worcestershire sauce
1/8 teaspoon crushed red pepper flakes
1 teaspoon arrowroot powder
Chopped parsley for garnish

Season meat pieces with salt and pepper, set aside. Heat 2 tablespoons olive oil on medium high heat in a large sauté pan until shimmering. Cook mushrooms and onions for approximately 12-15 minutes, until soft, stirring occasionally. Season liberally with salt and pepper. Remove mushrooms and onions from pan and set aside on a plate. Place pan back on medium high heat, add remaining 2 tablespoons of olive oil to the same pan until shimmering. Sear the meat pieces until browned on all sides. Add mushrooms and onions back into the sauté pan with the seared meat. In a mixing bowl, whisk together 1 cup water, coconut cream, dairy free plain yogurt, minced garlic, tomato paste, Worcestershire sauce, crushed red pepper flakes, arrowroot powder, 1 teaspoon salt, and 1/4 teaspoon pepper. Add mixture to pan, stirring in well. Bring to a boil and then turn down to a simmer. Cover, leaving lid partially open to allow steam to escape so the liquid will reduce. Simmer approximately 1½-2 hours, or until the meat is tender and can be cut with a fork. While simmering, check the mixture every 20-30 minutes and season with salt and pepper. Serve garnished with chopped parsley.

Pork Belly

(Serves 4-6)

To Prepare The Pork Belly:
1 bay leaf
1 teaspoon dried thyme
2 tablespoons salt
2-3 pound pork belly

Marinade:
2 tablespoons gluten free soy sauce
1 teaspoon dried mustard
1 teaspoon salt, plus extra for pork belly skin
1 teaspoon dried rosemary
1 teaspoon minced garlic
1/2 teaspoon Chinese five spice
1/2 teaspoon fresh pepper

In a large pot, bring water, bay leaf, thyme, and salt to a boil. Add pork belly and boil for 20 minutes. Remove pork from water and pat dry. Season with salt and pepper, let cool, and then refrigerate over night, uncovered.

Preheat oven to 350°. Poke fatty skin side of pork belly repeatedly with a fork until the entire surface of the fatty skin has been pierced, being careful not to pierce the meat. In a small bowl, whisk together soy sauce, dried mustard, salt, dried rosemary, minced garlic, Chinese five spice, and fresh pepper. Pour marinade onto the meat side of the pork belly, dredging it. Place the meat side of the pork belly face down into a roasting pan, letting the excess marinade drip into the roasting pan. Liberally salt the fatty skin side, and place in oven. Let cook for 30-45 minutes, or until the skin starts to get golden. Turn the oven up to 500°, and let the skin finish becoming crispy and browned, about another 20-30 minutes. Remove pork belly from oven and let stand 5-10 minutes. Slice pieces of pork belly and serve with drippings from the pan.

Sunday Funday Herb-Coated Standing Rib Roast

(Serves 8-10)

1 6-8 pound bone-in rib roast
Salt and pepper
1 teaspoon fresh thyme leaves
1 teaspoon fresh rosemary leaves, chopped
2 tablespoons Dijon mustard
1 tablespoon prepared horseradish
1 tablespoon olive oil
1 teaspoon garlic powder
1 teaspoon salt
1/2 teaspoon fresh pepper

Let rib roast rest outside of fridge for 1 hour before cooking. Place rib roast, bone side down, in the roasting pan. Preheat oven to 450°. Season roast liberally with salt and pepper. Whisk together remaining ingredients into a sauce. Spread the sauce over the top and sides of the rib roast until everything is coated. Place in oven and cook for 20 minutes, then reduce oven heat to 350° and cook for additional 1½-2 hours until a meat thermometer inserted reads 140-160° for rare to medium. Remove from oven, let stand for 20-30 minutes. Rib roast will continue to cook while standing. Carve rib roast along bone, lengthwise to serve.

Asparagus Swiss Stuffed Meatloaf

(Serves 4)

When is meatloaf not a boring ol' meatloaf? When it's stuffed with asparagus and Swiss cheese! If you want to be fancy, you can use the Homemade Ketchup (p. 224) recipe in place of the glaze.

1 pound ground beef
1 pound ground pork
1 teaspoon salt
1/2 teaspoon pepper
1/2 teaspoon garlic powder
1 medium sweet onion, finely chopped
1/2 cup almond flour
1 egg
1/2 cup parmesan, freshly grated, plus more for garnish
1 tablespoon tomato paste
1 teaspoon fresh basil, finely chopped
1 teaspoon parsley, finely chopped
Olive oil spray for pan
10-14 asparagus stalks, rough ends trimmed and discarded
4 slices Swiss cheese

Glaze:
4 tablespoons tomato paste
1 soft pitted date, pulverized (optional)
1/4 cup water, plus more if necessary
2 teaspoons Dijon mustard
2 teaspoons balsamic vinegar

Preheat oven to 375°. In a large mixing bowl, combine beef, pork, salt, pepper, garlic powder, chopped onion, almond flour, egg, parmesan, tomato paste, basil, and parsley, combining with your hands until well mixed. Separate into two even sections. Spray a 4x8 meatloaf pan with olive oil spray. Press first half of meatloaf into loaf pan.

In a small mixing bowl, whisk together glaze ingredients. If it's too thick, add more water 1 tablespoon at a time. Brush half of glaze onto meat in the loaf pan.

Lay asparagus stalks lengthwise atop glazed meat. Lay Swiss cheese slices atop asparagus. Press remaining meatloaf mixture into loaf pan, flattening the top. Spread remaining glaze evenly atop meatloaf.

Bake in oven 1 hour until meat loaf is done through. Remove from oven and let stand 10 minutes. Cut into slices and serve.

Braised Short Rib Grinders

(Yields 6-8 portions)

The following three recipes are sandwich-inspired, where you can enjoy the tasty, meaty, sandwich innards without feeling like you're missing the bread. If you insist on bookending with bread, and wanna keep it low carb, I humbly suggest the Bagel Rounds on page 200.

---

1 sweet onion, chopped
1 cup plus 1 tablespoon red wine vinegar, divided
2-3 pounds boneless beef short ribs
Salt and pepper
2 slices bacon, chopped
4 sprigs thyme
1/2 cup chicken broth
1 tablespoon whole grain mustard
1 teaspoon onion powder
6-8 slices cheddar cheese
2 tablespoons prepared horseradish
1/2 cup crème fraîche or sour cream
1 tablespoon chopped fresh chives

In a mixing bowl, place chopped onion. Pour over 1 cup of red wine vinegar. Cover with plastic wrap and put in fridge while the rest of the meal is preparing.

Place short ribs in slow cooker, season liberally with salt and pepper. Spread bacon pieces over short ribs, then place thyme sprigs over ribs. In a small mixing bowl, whisk together chicken broth, whole grain mustard, onion powder, and remaining tablespoon of red wine vinegar. Pour over ribs. Cover and cook for 2-3 hours on high in slow cooker, or until ribs are fall apart tender.

Preheat oven to 350°. Remove ribs from liquid, chop up, and separate into 6-8 portions placed on a foil-lined baking sheet. Cover each portion with a slice of cheddar. Bake in oven for 5-8 minutes, or until cheese is fully melted over the ribs. In a small bowl, whisk together horseradish and crème fraîche. Remove from oven, using a spatula to gently move each portion onto plates. Garnish with pickled onions strained from red wine vinegar from fridge, horseradish cream, and fresh chives. Serve immediately.

PHILLY CHEESESTEAKS

(Yields 8-10 portions)

2-3 pounds boneless top sirloin steak
Salt and pepper
1 tablespoon olive oil
2 onions, sliced
4 bell peppers, sliced (use a variety of colors)
1/2 teaspoon onion powder
1/2 teaspoon garlic powder
10 slices provolone, American cheese, or a mixture of both
Banana peppers, for garnish
Tomato, chopped for garnish
Mayonnaise, for garnish
Mustard, for garnish

Put sirloin steak in the freezer for 2-3 hours until hardened, but not frozen solid. Remove from freezer and slice very thinly, cutting out and discarding any hard pieces of gristle. Season cut pieces of steak well with salt and pepper.

In a large flat-bottomed sauté pan, heat olive oil on medium high heat until shimmering. Sauté onions and peppers, tossing to coat with oil. Stir in onion powder and garlic powder, season with salt and pepper, cover and reduce heat to low. Let simmer for 15-20 minutes, or until onions and peppers are soft.

Heat a large nonstick griddle pan or large sauté pan to medium high heat and cook cut steak, using a spatula to flip the meat. Season once with salt and pepper as you cook the meat. Add in the peppers and onions, tossing with the steak pieces, season once more with salt and pepper. Separate the steak mixture into 8-10 portions and melt cheese atop each portion. Remove each portion from heat and serve on a salad or on a plate garnished with banana peppers, chopped tomato, mayonnaise, and mustard.

Turkey Reuben Roll Ups

Sliced deli turkey
Homemade Thousand Island Dressing
Sauerkraut
Swiss cheese, thinly sliced

Preheat oven or toaster oven to 325°. Lay two slices of turkey flat on toaster oven tray or baking sheet. Pour one thin layer of thousand island. Cover with a layer of sauerkraut, then a slice of cheese, keeping everything level. Pop into toaster oven or regular oven for 10 minutes, or until cheese is melted. Cover with one final layer of thousand island, roll up, and serve.

Homemade Thousand Island Dressing

(Yields 1 cup)

So many store-bought dressings have so many bad oils, chemicals, and preservatives in them. Take control by making your own. Use the Homemade Ketchup recipe (p. 224) in this Thousand Island Dressing to limit the sugar even more.

3/4 cup mayonnaise
2 tablespoons ketchup
1/2 teaspoon minced garlic
1 tablespoon hot sauce
2 tablespoons minced onion
1/2 dill pickle spear, cut into chunks
Salt and pepper to taste

Put all ingredients into a food processor, blender, or Vitamix and pulse until desired level of creaminess.

PORK CHOP SCHNITZEL WITH MUSHROOM SAUCE

(Serves 3-4)

1 pound boneless pork chops, pounded to 1/4" thickness
Salt and pepper
2 tablespoons olive oil
1 egg
1 cup almond flour
2 tablespoons butter
2 teaspoons thyme leaves
1 cup beef broth
1 pound baby bella or cremini mushrooms, sliced
1 teaspoon arrowroot powder
1 tablespoon water

Season the thin pork cutlets with salt and pepper. Heat the olive oil in a large flat-bottomed nonstick sauté pan to medium high heat, until shimmering. Whisk the egg in a shallow dish and pour almond flour onto a flat dish. Dredge each cutlet in egg and then dip into almond flour, covering each side. Place in heated pan and cook 8-10 minutes or until browned, turning halfway through. Remove pork from heat and let rest on a plate. Add butter and thyme to the pan, and after the butter melts add in beef broth, bringing it to a low boil. Add mushrooms, then salt and pepper to taste and continue to simmer at a low boil for 10-12 minutes, stirring occasionally. In a small bowl, mix the arrowroot powder with 1 tablespoon of water until dissolved and then pour into center of pan, whisking as you pour. Remove pan from heat, and if the mixture is too thick add more water a 1 tablespoon at a time. Pour mushrooms atop pork cutlets and serve immediately.

Shake and Bake Pork Chops

(Serves 4-6)

2 pounds thin cut boneless pork chops
Salt and pepper
1 tablespoon stone ground mustard

Coating:
1½ cups almond flour
1/2 cup freshly grated parmesan
1 tablespoon minced fresh parsley
1 teaspoon minced fresh jalapeño
1 teaspoon dried mustard
1 teaspoon onion powder
1 teaspoon salt
1/2 teaspoon ground white pepper

Preheat oven to 350°. Dry off pork chops thoroughly with a paper towel. Season pork chops with salt and pepper and lay evenly on a parchment lined baking sheet. Using a pastry or silicon brush, spread a thin layer of ground mustard on both sides of pork chops. In a food processor or Vitamix, pulse almond flour, parmesan, minced parsley, minced jalapeño, dried mustard, onion powder, salt, and white pepper until finely ground, about 20-30 seconds. Pour dried mixture into a large plastic baggie. Shake coated pork chops, 1-2 at a time, in plastic baggie to coat. Lay on parchment-lined baking sheet. Bake in oven 15-20 minutes or until done through. Serve immediately.

BACON WRAPPED PORK TENDERLOIN

(Serves 4-6)

2 pound pork tenderloin (or two 1 pound tenderloins), trimmed of excess fat
Salt and pepper
2 tablespoons Dijon mustard
2 tablespoons fresh squeezed orange juice
6-8 slices of bacon, trimmed to wrap around pork tenderloins
2 rosemary sprigs

Preheat oven to 400°. Place pork tenderloin on a foil-lined baking sheet, season with salt and pepper. In a small mixing bowl, whisk together Dijon mustard and orange juice. Spread mixture over pork. Gently wrap pork evenly with bacon pieces. Put in oven and cook for 15 minutes. Add rosemary sprigs alongside pork, turn up heat to broil. Cook an additional 5-7 minutes until pork is done to an internal temperature of 165-170°, and bacon on outside is crispy. Remove from oven, slice, and serve.

Homemade Sausage, Part One: Hot Italian Sausage

(Yields 8-9 2" patties)

1 tablespoon fresh minced oregano
2 teaspoons fresh minced rosemary
2 teaspoons salt
1/2 teaspoon onion powder
1/2 teaspoon garlic powder
1/2 teaspoon paprika
1/2 teaspoon fennel seeds
1/2 teaspoon celery salt
1/4 teaspoon pepper flakes
1/4 teaspoon red pepper flakes (or more if you want more spicy)
1 pound ground pork, highest fat content available
1 tablespoon olive oil, back fat, or beef tallow for frying

Whisk together all herbs and spices in a small mixing bowl. Fold into ground pork and mix evenly. Heat olive oil, back fat, or beef tallow in a nonstick pan to medium high heat. Form pork into patties and cook thoroughly, about 4-5 minutes per side. Serve immediately or store in airtight container in fridge for up to 3 days to use in recipes that call for sausage.

Kielbasa with Sautéed Cabbage and Fennel

(Serves 4)

1/2 red or purple cabbage, stem removed
1 fennel bulb, thinly sliced
2 tablespoons olive oil
Salt and pepper
1/4 cup white vinegar
1/4 cup apple cider vinegar
2 small gala apples
1-2 pounds precooked Kielbasa (Polish sausage)

On the side of a box grater, grate cabbage until you have around 5-6 cups. Thinly slice fennel bulb, discarding tough end and green stems. In a large sauté pan or Le Creuset, heat olive oil to medium high heat, and sauté cabbage and fennel until hot and coated with olive oil. Season with salt and pepper. Cook for 10-12 minutes until soft. Add white vinegar and apple cider vinegar, seasoning again with salt and pepper. Cook an additional 5-6 minutes, season again with salt and pepper. Cover and reduce heat. Let cook an additional 5-7 minutes until soft. Season with salt and pepper again if necessary.

Heat grill to medium high heat (about 450°). Slice gala apples in half, remove and discard core, and cut each half once more into quarters. Grill apple slices and kielbasa until hot and charred. Remove from grill and slice kielbasa, serving with cooked cabbage and fennel mixture and garnished with a couple of apple slices.

Chicken Cauliflower Fried Rice

(Serves 4)

1/2 cup almonds, crushed into pieces
5 tablespoons coconut oil, divided
1 pound chicken breasts or thighs, cubed in 1/2"-inch pieces
Salt and pepper
1/4 teaspoon red pepper flakes
3 teaspoons gluten free soy sauce (or coconut aminos)
1 teaspoon grated fresh ginger, divided
1/2 medium onion, chopped
2 stalks celery, chopped
1/2 cup chopped baby carrots
8 ounces cremini or baby bella mushrooms, loosely chopped
1/2 cup frozen peas
1/3 cup dried cranberries
1 head of cauliflower, grated into rice
2 eggs
1 teaspoon fish sauce

Preheat oven to 350°. Spread crushed almond pieces on a foil-lined baking sheet evenly. Bake in oven 5-8 minutes until lightly toasted, being careful not to burn. Remove from oven and set aside.

In a medium sauté pan, heat 2 tablespoons of the coconut oil on medium high heat. Cook the chicken pieces until done, about 7-10 minutes. Season with salt, pepper, red pepper flakes, 1 teaspoon of the soy sauce, and 1/2 teaspoon of the fresh ginger. Remove from heat.

In a separate large sauté pan, heat 2 more tablespoons of coconut oil on medium high heat and sauté onions, celery, carrots, mushrooms, remaining fresh ginger, and 1 more teaspoon of soy sauce, until veggies are softened, about 5-6 minutes. Stir in peas, season with salt and pepper. Pour chicken pieces into veggie mix pan. Add cranberries and stir.

Move vegetables and chicken to the perimeter of the sauté pan, add remaining coconut oil, and sauté the cauliflower rice on medium high heat until the cauliflower rice starts to slightly brown, about 5 minutes. Season with salt and pepper. Let it sit in the skillet, then flip the cauliflower rice with a spatula a few times. Mix all ingredients, then push ingredients to the side to make an empty space in the center of the sauté pan. Crack two eggs in center space, scramble the eggs, and separate them into pieces. Fold egg pieces into entire mixture. Drizzle in remaining soy sauce and fish sauce, then mix. Add in toasted crushed almond pieces and serve. Season with additional soy sauce or salt and pepper to preferred taste.

Asian Fried Chicken Salad
(Serves 2)

Salad

1/3 cup slivered almonds
1 pound of thinly cut boneless, skinless chicken breasts
Salt and pepper
1 egg, beaten
1 cup almond flour
1/2 cup olive oil for frying
2 cups chopped hearts of romaine leaves
1 cup of pre cut broccoli or cabbage slaw (found bagged in produce section)
2 green onions, chopped

Sesame Mustard Dressing

(Yields enough dressing for two salads)

1/4 cup mayonnaise
1½ teaspoons rice vinegar
1/2 tablespoon Dijon mustard
1/4 teaspoon sesame oil or toasted sesame oil

Preheat oven to 350°. Toast slivered almonds on a baking sheet for 8-10 minutes or until browned and fragrant, being careful not to burn. Remove from oven and set aside.

Slice the chicken breasts lengthwise into 2" strips, season with salt and pepper. Dredge the chicken pieces in egg, then coat with almond flour. Heat olive oil in a large sauté pan on medium high heat until shimmering. Fry the coated chicken pieces, until done, about 3-4 minutes per side, being careful not to burn the almond flour coating. Remove from oil, let stand on paper towels to drain excess oil.

Divide the chopped romaine leaves, slaw, and green onions equally between two large salad bowls and top with toasted almonds. Slice chicken pieces into thin strips and place atop salads. Whisk together all dressing ingredients in a small mixing bowl. Drizzle dressing evenly over each salad and serve.

Balsamic Chicken with Kale Chopped Salad

(Serves 4)

Balsamic Chicken

1 pound thinly sliced chicken breasts
Salt and pepper
4 tablespoons olive oil, divided
Juice of half a lemon
1/2 tablespoon balsamic vinegar
1/2 tablespoon red wine vinegar
1/2 teaspoon garlic powder
1/2 teaspoon onion powder

On a plate, place chicken breasts and season with salt and pepper on both sides. In a large bowl, whisk together 3 tablespoons of the olive oil, the lemon juice, balsamic vinegar, red wine vinegar, garlic powder, onion powder, and additional salt and pepper.

Place chicken breasts in bowl, fully coat with marinade, and let sit for 15-20 minutes. In a large griddle pan, heat remaining 1 tablespoon of olive oil to medium high heat. Cook chicken breasts (discarding remaining marinade) until cooked through, about 4-5 minutes per side. Remove from heat and set aside.

KALE CHOPPED SALAD

1 cup quartered cherry tomatoes
1/2 cup chopped walnuts
2 avocados, peeled, pitted, and cut into half inch cubes
1/2 cup chopped mixed green and black olives
1 tablespoon chopped green onions
1/2 cup dried cranberries
Juice of half an orange
1/2 tablespoon balsamic vinegar
1/2 tablespoon red wine vinegar
1 large bunch of kale, hard center stems cut out and discarded, then chopped

In a large bowl, combine cherry tomatoes, walnuts, avocado cubes, olives, green onions, and cranberries. Toss with juice of half an orange, balsamic vinegar, and red wine vinegar, being careful not to smash the avocado cubes. Add in the chopped kale and toss ingredients well together.

Place one chicken breast on a salad plate, then place 1 cup of chopped salad on top. Repeat for remaining chicken breasts and salad and serve immediately.

White Balsamic Chicken Thighs

(Serves 2-4)

1-2 pounds boneless chicken thighs (preferably with skin-on)
Salt and pepper
2 tablespoons olive oil
1/4 cup white balsamic vinegar (or white wine vinegar)
1/4 cup chicken stock
1 tablespoon butter

Season chicken thighs well with salt and pepper. In a large sauté pan, heat olive oil to medium high heat, and cook thighs until done through, about 10-15 minutes, flipping halfway through. Remove thighs to a plate and set aside. In the same pan, still at medium high heat, pour in vinegar, scraping up brown chicken bits at the bottom of the pan while the vinegar sizzles. Add chicken stock, stirring thoroughly. Turn heat down to low, add butter, stirring until melted and blended. Add back in chicken thighs, dredging them on both sides in the vinegar sauce. Serve immediately.

CRISPY ORANGE CHICKEN THIGHS

(Serves 4)

Salt and pepper
2-3 pounds bone-in, skin-on chicken thighs
1/2 cup fresh squeezed orange juice (about 2-3 oranges)
1/4 cup gluten free soy sauce (or coconut aminos)
2 tablespoons white wine vinegar
1 teaspoon minced garlic
2 teaspoons grated fresh ginger
1/2 teaspoon ground mustard seed
2 tablespoons olive oil

Salt and pepper the chicken thighs. Whisk together remaining ingredients and marinate chicken thighs in marinade for 3-4 hours in the refrigerator.

Heat grill up to 450°. Discard marinade and cook thighs skin down for 10 minutes, flip and grill 5-10 minutes longer—until you can slice through and juices run clear or when inserting a meat thermometer the temperature is 180°.

If you'd like to cook thighs in the oven, heat oven to 425° and cook skin side up on a foil-lined baking sheet for 30-40 minutes or until you can slice through and juices run clear; or when inserting a meat thermometer, the temperature is 180°.

Villa Cappelli Chicken Cacciatore

(Serves 6-8)

Paul Cappelli and Steven Crutchfield are probably right this second hovered over an olive oil press in Puglia, Italy, so that the rest of us can treat ourselves to 100% real olive oil. If you haven't yet picked up some Villa Cappelli olive oil, please go do that immediately, then come back here and make this recipe, which is a Cappelli family specialty on which I've put my low carb spin.

---

1 pound bone-in, skin-on chicken thighs
1 pound skin-on chicken legs
Salt and pepper
2 tablespoons Villa Cappelli olive oil
1 medium onion, finely chopped
1 teaspoon minced garlic
2 tablespoons chopped sage leaves
1 cup diced tomatoes, puréed
1 tablespoon tomato paste (or Villa Cappelli sun dried tomato spread)
1 cup water
2 tablespoons white wine vinegar
1 cup pitted green olives, sliced
1 cup frozen peas

Season thighs and legs with salt and pepper. Heat olive oil to medium high heat in a large, flat-bottomed sauté pan until hot and shimmering. Brown chicken pieces, flipping halfway through, about 7-10 minutes a side. Remove chicken from heat. Add onions, garlic, sage, tomatoes, and tomato paste, also scraping up any chicken renderings sticking to the bottom of the pan. Season with salt and pepper. Cook, stirring infrequently, until onions are translucent, about 5-7 minutes. Add cup of water and white wine vinegar, stir to mix with onions. Add back in chicken pieces, dredge chicken with the sauce, season with salt and pepper. Bring sauce to boil. Cover, turn heat down to low, and let simmer for 15-20 minutes. Add in green olives and peas, gently stir to mix. Cover pan again, unless sauce is too watery, then leave uncovered, and let simmer another 15-20 minutes.

Lemon Orange Chicken

(Serves 3-4)

2 eggs
1/2 cup heavy cream
1 pound thin cut chicken breasts
Salt and pepper
1 cup almond flour
3/4 cup chicken broth
1/3 cup olive oil
Juice of half a lemon
1 teaspoon grated lemon zest, minced
Juice of half an orange

In a wide bowl, whisk together eggs and heavy cream. Season chicken breasts on both sides with salt and pepper. Pour almond flour into another wide bowl. Dredge chicken breasts, one at a time in the egg wash, and then coat the chicken in the almond flour. Heat olive oil in a large, flat-bottomed nonstick pan to medium high heat. Do the sizzle test by testing a pinch of almond flour in the oil, and if it sizzles, it's hot enough. Cook chicken about 7-9 minutes per side or until done through. Remove chicken breasts to a paper towel lined plate.

Pour chicken broth into pan, bring to a boil and use a silicon spatula to scrape up all the cooked drippings. Add lemon juice, zest, and orange juice, season with salt and pepper. Let cook an additional 2-3 minutes. Pour over chicken breasts and serve.

Tomato Basil Cod

(Serves 4-5)

1½ pounds heirloom or Roma tomatoes, chopped, discarding pulp/seeds
10 basil leaves, chopped
1 teaspoon minced garlic
Salt and pepper
2 tablespoons olive oil, divided
1½ pounds cod fillets

Preheat oven to 350°. In a 9"x12" Pyrex pan or other glass baking dish, spread around chopped tomatoes, basil leaves, and minced garlic, drizzle with 1 tablespoon of olive oil, and season with salt and pepper. Bake for 20-25 minutes, or until tomatoes are soft and skin starts to blister. Remove baking dish from oven and reduce heat to 300°.

Move tomato basil mixture to the sides of the baking dish, and place cod fillets side by side, tilting baking dish to allow the tomato juices to coat the cod edges slightly. Season cod with salt and pepper and drizzle with remaining tablespoon of olive oil. Bake for an additional 15 minutes until cod is done through, but not overdone/dry. Serve immediately.

Salmon Puttanesca

(Serves 4-5)

===

2 tablespoons olive oil, divided
1½ pounds salmon fillets
Salt and pepper, plus additional 1/2 teaspoon salt
1/2 medium onion, diced
1 teaspoon minced garlic
2 tablespoons capers
3/4 cup pitted black olives, chopped
1/2 teaspoon red pepper flakes
1/2 teaspoon onion powder
1/2 teaspoon fresh pepper
7-10 basil leaves, chopped
1 teaspoon fresh oregano leaves, chopped, plus additional for garnish
2 14-ounce cans diced tomatoes, one can puréed in blender or food processor
3 tablespoons tomato paste

===

Preheat oven to 350° or heat grill. Season salmon fillets with salt and pepper, drizzle baking pan with 1 tablespoon olive oil, then place salmon fillets, skin side down in baking dish. Bake 15-20 minutes until desired doneness. If grilling, oil grill grate and grill about 10 minutes, skin side down until desired doneness.

Meanwhile, in a saucepan on medium high heat, sauté the onion and garlic in remaining tablespoon of olive oil until soft, about 4-5 minutes. Add the capers, olives, red pepper flakes, 1/2 teaspoon salt, onion powder, basil leaves, and oregano leaves, stirring periodically for 2-3 minutes. Stir in the tomatoes and tomato paste, season with additional salt and pepper. Bring to a boil, then turn the heat down to low, letting sauce simmer for 15-20 minutes. Season once more with salt and pepper.

Serve in a shallow bowl, ladle one to two scoops of the sauce and place the salmon fillet on top. Garnish with fresh oregano leaves.

SALMON BURGERS

(Yields 4-5 burgers)

1/2 cup almond flour
Zest of 1 lemon, minced
1/2 cup mayonnaise, divided
1 egg
2 tablespoons finely chopped dill
1/4 onion, minced
1 pound wild caught salmon, cut from skin and into small pieces
Salt and pepper
2 tablespoons olive oil
Juice of half a lemon
Butter lettuce leaves
Sliced avocado

In a large bowl, whisk together almond flour, lemon zest, 1/4 cup of mayonnaise, egg, dill, and onion. Fold in salmon pieces and mix. Press into burger patties, lay flat on a large plate or baking sheet, and refrigerate for 20-30 minutes.

Heat olive oil in a cast iron pan or griddle on medium high heat, gently place salmon burgers clockwise in pan, cook for 4-5 minutes per side, gently flipping. Season with salt and pepper while cooking. Remove burgers to a paper towel lined plate.

Whisk together remaining 1/4 cup mayonnaise and the lemon juice. Serve salmon burgers wrapped in butter lettuce leaves with a dollop of lemon-mayo and avocado slices.

HALIBUT WITH PEAS AND MUSTARD SAUCE

(Serves 4-6)

2 pounds halibut fillets
1 tablespoon olive oil
Salt and pepper
1 shallot, finely chopped
1/2 cup of chicken broth
1/2 cup white wine vinegar
1 stick of butter,
cubed into 1-inch pieces
1 cup of frozen peas
1 tablespoon plus 1 teaspoon ground mustard
2 tablespoons fresh chives, finely chopped for garnish

Preheat oven to 400°. Place halibut fillets skin side down on a nonstick foil-lined baking sheet. Rub olive oil on halibut fillets, and season with salt and pepper. Bake fillets in oven for 12-15 minutes.

Meanwhile, in a medium sauce pan, combine shallots, chicken broth, and white wine vinegar, bringing to a boil. Reduce heat to medium low and simmer until liquid is reduced, about 10-12 minutes. Whisk in mustard, then butter, one piece at a time. Fold in peas, cooking 1 additional minute. Remove from heat and pour atop cooked halibut fillets. Garnish with chopped chives and serve immediately.

Seared Salmon with Caper Niçoise Dressing

(Serves 2)

2 salmon fillets
Salt and pepper
4 tablespoons olive oil, divided
1/2 pound haricots verts (little french green beans, or regular green beans)
1/2 tablespoon red wine vinegar
Juice of half a lemon, plus lemon wedges for garnish
1 teaspoon Dijon mustard
2 tablespoons capers
1/2 cup cherry tomatoes, halved
1/2 cup kalamata olives, pitted
2 Persian cucumbers, sliced (or 1 English cucumber)

Season salmon fillets well with salt and pepper. Heat 1 tablespoon of olive oil in a nonstick pan on medium high heat until hot and shimmering. Place salmon fillets skin side up and cook 2-3 minutes, seasoning skin with salt and pepper while cooking. Flip salmon and cook the skin well, about 3-4 minutes. Add more olive oil if necessary to sear the skin.

Steam the haricots verts in a steamer basket over medium high heat until bright green, about 4 minutes. Or microwave haricots verts in a bag about 4 minutes until bright green. Remove from basket and let cool slightly.

In a small mixing bowl, whisk together remaining 3 tablespoons of olive oil, red wine vinegar, lemon juice, Dijon mustard, and capers. Season with salt and pepper to taste. Toss cherry tomatoes, olives, and cucumber slices in half the dressing.

Place the salmon and haricots verts on the plate, drizzle with remaining dressing, top with vegetable mixture, splitting between the two plates. Serve immediately, garnish with lemon wedges.

TRICIA'S SEA BASS WITH AGRODOLCE SAUCE

Tricia Clark is a food stylist and food show producer. She's super smart, and I let her boss me around about all things food. Tricia is that friend that you can text about the ins and outs of toasting nuts and The Bachelor in the same text chain. I begged her to share some of her food wisdom with us in this book, and she did not disappoint. Agrodolce sauce is a traditional sweet and sour Italian sauce, but then Tricia added a twist with the addition of harissa, which is a mediterranean spice mix. If you do not have harissa paste or dried harissa, you can use red pepper flakes. For fish choices, you can use fillets of sea bass, halibut, black bass, or use a whole Thai snapper.

Agrodolce Sauce

(Yields enough sauce for 1 whole fish or 2 fillets)

1/4 cup dried cherries, chopped
1/4 cup sherry vinegar
1/3 cup olive oil
1/4 cup raw almonds, roughly chopped
2 small shallots cut into rings
1 teaspoon harissa paste (or 1 teaspoon dried harissa, pulverized in
one teaspoon of olive oil until a paste forms)
Salt to taste

Soak chopped dried cherries in sherry vinegar while preparing the nuts. In a sauté pan over medium heat, add the olive oil and almonds. Cook the almonds until the nuts start to turn a golden brown. Remove from heat and let cool.

Combine soaked cherries, shallots, and harissa paste. Add cooled nuts and oil. Season with salt to taste. Let stand in fridge 8 hours or overnight, bring to room temperature before serving with baked fish, below.

Fish

(Serves 2)

1 pound sea bass fillets, skin trimmed and discarded (usually 2 fillets)
Salt and pepper
Agrodolce Sauce, removed from fridge and brought to room temperature
Parsley, chopped for garnish

Preheat oven to 350°. Line a baking sheet with parchment paper. Place fish fillets on parchment paper. Season with salt and pepper. Cook in middle rack of oven for 12 minutes, until done through, being careful not to overcook. Remove from oven and set on plates, divide Agrodolce Sauce between two the two fillets, garnish with parsley and serve.

Coconut Mango Cauliflower "Rice" Salad with Grilled Shrimp

(Serves 4-5)

4 tablespoons olive oil, divided
1/2 onion, diced
2 16-ounce bags of cauliflower "rice" or 2 heads of cauliflower, grated
1 jalapeño, deseeded and finely chopped
Salt and pepper
Zest of 1 lime, minced
Juice of 1 lime
1/4 cup coconut milk
1/2 teaspoon salt
1/4 teaspoon pepper
1 mango, cored, peeled, and cubed
2 tablespoons fresh mint, chopped
2 pounds peeled, deveined shrimp

In a large sauté pan, heat 1 tablespoon olive oil on medium high heat. Sauté onion until soft, about 3-5 minutes. Add cauliflower rice and jalapeño, season with salt and pepper. Cook for 5-10 minutes, stirring occasionally. The cauliflower rice will release water as it cooks, water will eventually evaporate, and the rice will stick to the pan. Do not let the cauliflower rice burn, but it is okay to let it stick before stirring.

In a large bowl, whisk together remaining 3 tablespoons olive oil, lime zest, lime juice, coconut milk, salt, and pepper. Fold in mango cubes and mint. Then fold in cauliflower rice mix, letting the sauce get mixed in well with the cauliflower.

Preheat grill and soak bamboo skewers in water for ten minutes, then thread the shrimp, 4-5 per skewer, while grill heats. Season shrimp skewers with salt and pepper. Grill shrimp, 2-3 minutes on each side, until they are cooked through. Plate the cauliflower rice mixture and serve the shrimp on top.

Dinner Chopped Salad

(Yields 2 large salads)

3 pieces bacon
2 cups pre-cut cauliflower "rice" or 1 head cauliflower, grated into "rice"
1 tablespoon olive oil
1 firm avocado, peeled and pitted, cut into 1/2" slices
1/2 cup pumpkin seeds
Salt and pepper
1/2 cup butter
1/2 pound shrimp, peeled and deveined, tails removed
1 cup cherry or grape tomatoes, quartered
1 golden beet, peel discarded, chopped
2 cups baby arugula, chopped
2 cups baby spinach, chopped
Ranch Dressing (p. 220)

Cook bacon until crispy in a large nonstick sauté pan on medium high heat. Remove bacon to let drain on a paper towel, chop into pieces, and reserve bacon drippings in pan. Using the same pan, cook cauliflower rice on medium high heat until browned and crispy, about 10 minutes. Remove cauliflower rice and let cool on a plate. Turn heat down to medium, add olive oil to the remaining reserved bacon drippings in the pan, and fry avocado slices until browned on both sides, about 1-2 minutes per side. Gently remove avocado from heat and let cool. Turn heat in pan to low, and toast the pumpkin seeds about 3-4 minutes. Remove to paper towel to cool and season with salt and pepper.

In a small saucepan, heat butter to medium heat, until bubbling, add half of shrimp, tossing to make sure shrimp is coated in butter. Cook shrimp 3-5 minutes, remove from heat, pour in a bowl, and season with salt and pepper. Repeat with remaining half of shrimp. Chop shrimp into bite-sized pieces.

Arrange half of baby arugula and baby spinach on plates with half each of shrimp, cauliflower rice, tomatoes, chopped beets, fried avocado slices, toasted pumpkin seeds, and bacon pieces. Serve with a side of Ranch Dressing (p. 220).

SCALLOPS OVER BRAISED FENNEL AND WILTED SPINACH

(Serves 2-3 dinner portions or 4-5 starter portions)

1½ pounds large sea scallops
Salt and pepper
2 tablespoons olive oil, divided
2 fennel bulbs, tops and bottoms discarded and thinly sliced
1/4 cup chicken broth
1 tablespoon apple cider vinegar
1 tablespoon Dijon mustard
4 cups baby spinach leaves
1 pink grapefruit, segmented

Dry scallops with paper towel and season with salt and pepper, set aside.

In a large sauté pan, heat up 1 tablespoon of olive oil on medium high heat until oil is shimmering. Add in the fennel slices, season with salt and pepper, toss in the oil, and cook until starting to get soft, about 6-8 minutes. Add in chicken broth, apple cider vinegar, and Dijon mustard and toss. Season again with salt and pepper, cover, and continue to cook an additional 8-10 minutes. Remove lid and add in spinach and toss until wilted. Season once more with salt and pepper.

In a separate large nonstick pan, heat up remaining olive oil on medium heat until pan is hot and oil is shimmering. Cook scallops for 1-2 minutes per side, remove to a plate, and cover with foil.

Make 2-3 dinner plates or 4-5 salad plates dividing fennel-spinach mixture evenly. Top with scallops and garnish with pink grapefruit wedges. Serve immediately.

POKE BOWLS

(Serves 4)

With the proliferation of poke restaurants all over the US, the temptation of poke is everywhere. I know you can get the bowls with greens instead of rice if you want to keep it low carb, but for everyone who is trying to avoid gluten and added sugars, poke restaurants are gluten and sugar bombs. Make a poke bowl at home and control the environment by making a killer cauliflower rice, using coconut aminos or gluten free soy sauce, and creating your own wasabi mayo (which you can make entirely homemade or use your favorite sugar free store bought mayo). You can make nori flakes out of toasted seaweed sheets by cutting them up.

NORI CAULIFLOWER RICE

3 tablespoons olive oil
1/2 teaspoon sesame oil
1 teaspoon garlic powder
2 10-12 ounce bags of cauliflower "rice," or 1 head cauliflower, grated into "rice"
2 teaspoons salt
2 tablespoons nori flakes (cut from toasted seaweed sheets)
1 tablespoon coconut aminos or gluten free soy sauce

Heat olive oil, sesame oil, and garlic powder on medium heat in a large nonstick sauté pan. Cook cauliflower rice 5-10 minutes until it begins to soften, stirring often. Add salt. Turn heat down to low. Stir in nori flakes and coconut aminos. Continue to cook on low an additional 5-10 minutes until cooked but not browned, being careful not to overcook into mush.

Cucumber Salad

2 persian cucumbers, thinly sliced
3 radishes, thinly sliced
1 tablespoon chopped green onions, white part only, reserving green part for
poke bowl garnish
2 tablespoons white wine vinegar or rice wine vinegar
1 soft date, pitted, peeled, and pulverized into 1 tablespoon water
1/2 teaspoon sesame oil
2 teaspoons coconut aminos

Toss all ingredients in a small mixing bowl.

Poke Bowls

1 cup snap peas
1/2 cup mayonnaise
1 tablespoon wasabi paste
Nori Cauliflower Rice
Cucumber Salad
1 pound sashimi grade salmon or tuna steak, skin removed and diced
1 avocado, peeled, pitted, and sliced
2 teaspoons sesame seeds
2 tablespoons nori flakes (cut from toasted seaweed sheets)
2 green onions, green part chopped for garnish
Soy sauce or coconut aminos for garnish

Boil a large pot of water. Prepare an ice bath in a large mixing bowl. Blanch the snap peas for 30 seconds in boiling water, making sure all of them are immersed. Using a slotted spoon, remove snap peas and immediately place in ice bath to cool for 20 minutes. Dry off snap peas, trim each end, cut up the center line and remove peas. Cut on the diagonal, then set aside. In a small mixing bowl, whisk together mayonnaise and wasabi paste.

Assemble poke bowls: Divide cauliflower rice, cucumber salad, salmon, and avocado into four bowls. Garnish each with sesame seeds, nori flakes, green onions, soy sauce, snap peas, and wasabi mayo. Serve immediately.

Mushroom and Onion Bison Burgers

(Yields 4 burgers)

1 pound ground bison (or whatever ground meat you choose)
1/4 cup cremini mushrooms, minced, plus 1 cup sliced mushrooms
1/4 cup minced onion, plus 1 onion thinly sliced
1 teaspoon ground mustard
1/2 teaspoon yellow mustard
1/2 teaspoon onion powder
1 teaspoon salt
1/2 teaspoon pepper
2 tablespoons olive oil
1 teaspoon minced garlic
4 slices cheddar cheese (optional)
1 tomato, sliced
Butter lettuce or red leaf for wrapping

Place ground bison, 1/4 cup minced mushrooms, 1/4 cup minced onions, ground mustard, yellow mustard, onion powder, salt, and pepper into a large mixing bowl. Blend well with hands and form into 4 even burger patties, carefully shaping them. Heat olive oil in a cast iron skillet to medium high heat. Cook burgers until done through, about 3-4 minutes per side. Remove burgers to a plate, cover with foil. Keeping drippings in the pan, cook remaining onion slices, mushroom slices, minced garlic, and a pinch of salt and pepper, tossing onions and mushrooms in pan drippings. Turn heat down to medium low, cover and let cook for 5-8 minutes until onions and mushrooms are cooked through. Serve burgers with optional cheddar cheese slices, tomato slices, topped with onion and mushroom, wrapped in lettuce.

Soups, Slow Cooker, Instant Pot, and Casseroles

Pork Chops with Apples and Cinnamon

(Serves 4)

4 bone-in 1/2" thick pork chops
Salt and pepper
1 tablespoon olive oil
1 yellow, brown, or sweet onion, thinly sliced
1 teaspoon minced garlic
1 apple, peeled, cored, and thinly sliced
1 teaspoon cinnamon
1/4 cup chicken broth

Season pork chops with salt and pepper, set aside.

Instant Pot Directions:

Turn Instant Pot to Sauté setting, add olive oil and sauté onions in olive oil until soft, about 3-5 minutes. Add garlic, toss, and cook one more minute. Add apple slices and cinnamon, toss and sauté for an additional 2 minutes. Pour in chicken broth, season with salt and pepper, stir, and let sauté one more minute.

Add in pork chops, put on lid, and turn to Manual setting (on high pressure) for 3 minutes. Make sure valve seal on lid is in the "Sealed" position. After Manual cycle completes 3 minutes, continue to cook for 8 minutes, then flip the valve seal on the lid to "Release" to release remaining pressure. Make sure float valve has fully descended and open lid. Chops should be done through, or insert a meat thermometer to make sure it's 145-160°. Serve immediately, topped with onion and apple mixture.

Slow Cooker Directions:

Heat up oil in sauté pan to medium high, sauté onions in olive oil until soft, about 3-5 minutes. Add garlic, toss, and cook one more minute. Add apple slices and cinnamon, toss and sauté for an additional 2 minutes. Pour in chicken broth, season with salt and pepper, stir, and let sauté one more minute.

Pour entire mixture into slow cooker and add in pork chops. Cover and cook on high for 3-4 hours. Serve topped with onion and apple mixture.

Pork Tenderloin with Cranberries and Rosemary

(Serves 8)

2-3 pounds pork tenderloin, trimmed of excess fat (usually 2 tenderloins)
3 teaspoons salt, divided
1 teaspoon garlic powder
1 teaspoon onion powder
1 teaspoon ground white pepper, divided
1/8 teaspoon ground cayenne pepper
2 tablespoons olive oil
1/2 cup dried cranberries
1/4 cup chicken broth
1/4 cup balsamic vinegar
2 teaspoons minced garlic
3 tablespoons chopped rosemary leaves

Pat dry pork tenderloins. Whisk together 2 teaspoons salt, garlic powder, onion powder, 1/2 teaspoon white pepper, and ground cayenne, rub all over pork tenderloins.

Heat olive oil in a large sauté pan to medium high heat. Brown all sides of pork tenderloins, about 2 minutes per side. Remove from pan and place in Instant Pot or slow cooker.

Instant Pot Directions:

Place browned pork tenderloins into Instant Pot. In a mixing bowl, whisk together cranberries, chicken broth, balsamic vinegar, minced garlic, rosemary leaves, remaining 1 teaspoon salt, and remaining 1/2 teaspoon white pepper. Pour over pork tenderloin. Place lid on Instant Pot with the vent set to "Sealing." Cook on manual for 20 minutes. When manual cycle has run its course, let pressure release naturally for 10 minutes, then move vent to "Venting" for a quick release of pressure. When metal float valve has dropped, remove lid. Remove tenderloin from Instant Pot and let rest 5-7 minutes. Slice and serve topped with extra cranberries/juices from the Instant Pot.

Slow Cooker Directions:

Place browned pork tenderloins into slow cooker. In a mixing bowl, whisk together cranberries, chicken broth, balsamic vinegar, minced garlic, rosemary leaves, remaining 1 teaspoon salt, and remaining 1/2 teaspoon white pepper. Pour over pork tenderloin. Place lid on slow cooker and cook on low for 4 hours. Remove tenderloin from slow cooker and let rest 5-7 minutes. Slice and serve topped with extra cranberries/juices from the slow cooker.

INSTANT POT CHICKEN PAPRIKASH STEW

(Serves 4-6)

2-3 pounds skin-on, bone-in chicken thighs
Salt and pepper
1 tablespoon olive oil
1 red pepper, chopped
1 onion, chopped
2 teaspoons garlic
1½ tablespoons paprika
1/2 tablespoon smoked paprika
1 teaspoon onion powder
1 14-ounce can diced tomatoes
Sour cream, for garnish

Season chicken thighs liberally with salt and pepper. On Sauté setting of Instant Pot, heat olive oil until shimmering and sauté pepper and onion until soft, about 3-4 minutes. Add garlic, sauté 1-2 more minutes. Add paprika, smoked paprika, and onion powder, mixing into vegetables. Add chicken thighs, skin side down, and let brown 3-4 minutes. Stir in diced tomatoes. Place lid on Instant Pot, turn on Manual setting for 20 minutes with vent on "Sealing" setting. Let the setting run its course, waiting for the pressure valve to descend before opening the Instant Pot lid. Remove lid and take out chicken thighs, put them on a plate, and cover with foil. Turn Instant Pot to Sauté setting, bring sauce to boil and let reduce for 8-10 minutes. Plate chicken thighs, pour sauce over them and serve, garnished with sour cream if desired.

Instant Pot Red Curry Short Ribs

(Serves 3-4)

===

2-3 pounds boneless short ribs, cut into 1-2" chunks
Salt and pepper
2 tablespoons olive oil, divided
1/2 sweet onion, diced
1 teaspoon grated fresh ginger
1 teaspoon minced garlic
4 tablespoons sugar free red curry paste, divided
1 14-ounce can full fat coconut cream, water separated and discarded
2 teaspoons fish sauce, divided
2 teaspoons gluten free soy sauce or coconut aminos, divided
1 eggplant, cut into 1-inch chunks
1 red bell pepper cut into 1-inch pieces
1 cup chopped green beans, cut into 1-inch pieces
1/4 cup basil, chopped, plus more for garnish

===

Season short ribs with salt and pepper. Place Instant Pot on Sauté setting, heat 1 tablespoon olive oil on medium high heat until shimmering. Brown the short rib pieces, remove from pot. You may need to do this in batches depending on how many short ribs you have.

Add remaining tablespoon olive oil to Instant Pot. Sauté onions, ginger, and garlic until soft and aromatic, about 3-4 minutes. Season with salt and pepper. Add 2 tablespoons red curry paste, coconut cream, 1 teaspoon fish sauce, and 1 teaspoon soy sauce, whisk to blend. Add back in short rib pieces, stirring to coat with red curry sauce.

Cover Instant Pot with lid and lock, placing vent to "Sealing." Cook on Manual for 20 minutes. After Manual cycle completes, wait until the metal float valve descends (about 30 minutes), then open the lid and remove the short ribs, leaving the liquid in the Instant Pot.

Turn Instant Pot back to Sauté setting. Add remaining red curry paste, teaspoon fish sauce, and teaspoon soy sauce; whisk together. Add in eggplant, bell pepper, and green beans, let sauté for 10-15 minutes, stirring veggies every few minutes. The red curry sauce will reduce until creamy. Add in basil, sautéing 1-2 more minutes. Put short ribs back into red curry vegetable mixture, tossing until mixed and serve, garnished with additional chopped basil.

Slow Cooker Ropa Vieja (Flank Steak Stew)

(Serves 8-10)

2 tablespoons olive oil
2 sweet onions, thinly sliced
2 red bell peppers, thinly sliced
Salt and pepper
3 tablespoons tomato paste
2 teaspoons minced garlic
1½ teaspoons ground cumin
2 teaspoons dried oregano
1/4 cup chicken broth
1/4 cup white wine vinegar
2-3 bay leaves
2 pound flank steak, cut into 2" strips
1/2 cup sliced green olives

In a large sauté pan, heat olive oil to medium high heat until pan is hot and oil is shimmering. Add onions and peppers and cook until soft, about 8-10 minutes. Season with salt and pepper. Meanwhile, in a smaller mixing bowl, whisk together tomato paste, garlic, cumin, and oregano. Fold the tomato paste mixture into the onions and peppers, tossing to coat all the pieces. Pour in chicken broth and white wine vinegar and let cook an additional 4-5 minutes, until liquid has almost evaporated. Season again with salt and pepper. Pour entire contents of saucepan into a slow cooker. Add in bay leaves.

Season the flank steak strips liberally with salt and pepper. Tuck the flank steak strips into the onion and pepper mixture, coating them and making sure they're submerged in the mixture. Cook on low for 5-6 hours. After cooking, remove and discard bay leaves. Remove flank steak strips and cut strips into smaller 1/4"-1/2" pieces. Put flank steak pieces back into slow cooker. Add olive slices and toss. Serve immediately.

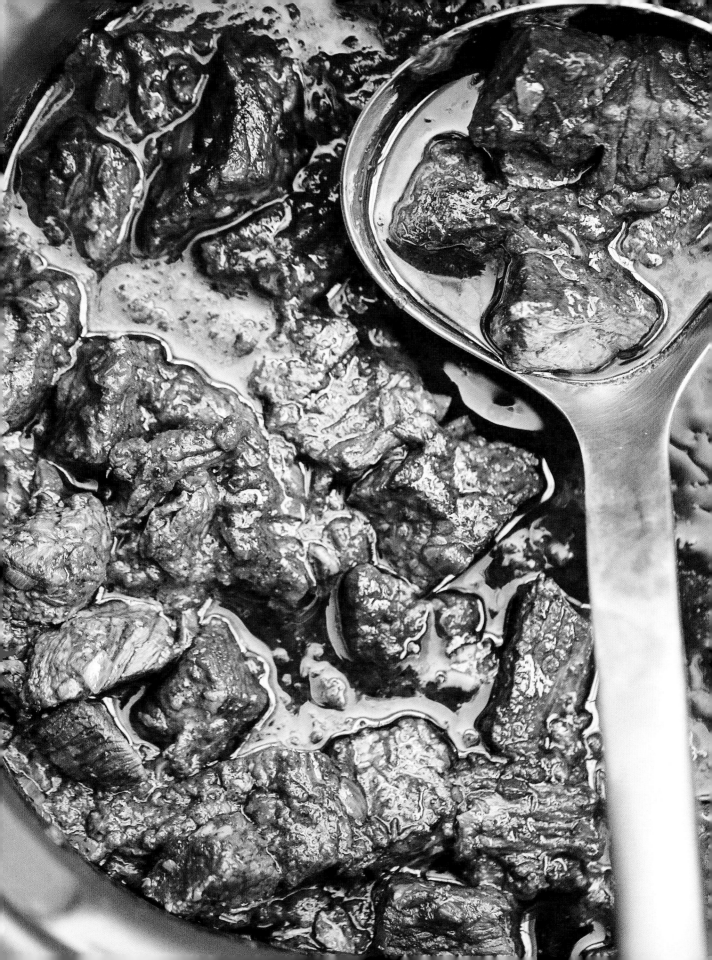

Red and Green Chili Chili

(Serves 4-6)

Usually chili gets its red color from tomatoes. Not this chili. This beautiful, bright, spicy chili is Texan/Southwestern style that uses a handpicked amalgam of peppers that strike your fancy at the grocery store. You can add in spicy peppers or keep it mild. Your choice.

2-4 pound chuck roast, trimmed of excess fat, cut into 1" cubes
Salt and pepper
6 red and green chili peppers
(I use a mixture of red jalapeño, Hatch chilis, and poblano peppers)
1 tablespoon olive oil
1 small onion, diced
Spice mix (see below)
2 cups beef or chicken broth
Sour cream for serving
Shredded cheddar for serving

Spice Mix:
1 tablespoon ground ancho chili pepper
1 teaspoon salt
1/2 teaspoon ground white pepper
1/2 teaspoon smoked paprika
1/2 teaspoon cumin
1/8 teaspoon ground cayenne

Preheat oven to 400°. Season chuck roast cubes with salt and pepper, set aside. Place 5 out of the 6 red and green chili peppers on a baking sheet and roast for 15 minutes, flipping peppers halfway through. Remove from oven and let cool. Peel skin from peppers, discard pepper tops and most of the seeds, depending on your taste. The more seeds left in, the more spicy the end result. De-stem and de-seed remaining fresh pepper. Place roasted peppers and fresh pepper into a small food processor or strong blender and pulse to a paste, scraping down sides as necessary.

In a large, flat-bottomed sauté pan, or in a slow cooker that has a sauté setting, heat olive oil to medium high heat and cook onions until soft, about 5 minutes. Whisk together spice mix in a small mixing bowl. Add beef cubes to pan, and sprinkle spice mix over beef cubes, tossing to coat. Let beef cubes brown, about 2 minutes per side, then remove to slow cooker on high setting (or turn slow cooker to high setting if using a multi-function slow cooker). Add in chili pepper paste, tossing with beef cubes. Add in broth, season with salt and pepper, cover, and let cook on high for 3 hours. Serve garnished with sour cream and shredded cheddar.

Ginger Garlic Sesame Pot Roast

(Serves 4-6)

On its own, the Ginger Garlic Sesame Vinaigrette that comprises the braising liquid for this pot roast dish makes a fantastic dressing for a Chinese chicken salad or a marinade for veggies/ chicken/fish to put on the grill. But in this case, we're going to take all the yumminess and let it cook a chuck roast into a tender, fall apart stew. Serve this with the Ginger Cilantro Cauliflower Rice dish from Eat Happy.

Toasted Sesame Paste

2 tablespoons sesame seeds

In a small nonstick sauté pan on medium high heat, toast sesame seeds until browned and toasted, tossing frequently, about 2-3 minutes. Be careful not to burn the delicate seeds. Pour seeds into a food processor or Vitamix and grind for 2-3 minutes, until a paste forms. You may need to scrape down the sides of the food processor a few times during this process. Use 1/2 teaspoon for the recipe below, and keep the rest airtight in the fridge for up to 2 weeks.

Ginger Garlic Sesame Vinaigrette

2/3 cup coconut aminos or gluten free soy sauce
1/3 cup balsamic vinegar
2 teaspoons grated fresh ginger
2 teaspoons minced garlic
1/2 teaspoon toasted sesame paste (see above)
1/2 teaspoon Chinese five spice

In a small mixing bowl, whisk all ingredients together.

GINGER GARLIC SESAME POT ROAST

2-3 pound chuck roast or rump roast
Salt and pepper
Large sweet onion, sliced
Ginger Garlic Sesame Vinaigrette

Season chuck roast with salt and pepper. Heat a large nonstick sauté pan to medium high heat. Brown all sides of roast, about 2-3 minutes per side. Place onion slices in slow cooker, place roast atop onions. Pour ginger garlic sesame vinaigrette over pot roast and onions. Cover; let cook in slow cooker 6-8 hours on low setting, until meat is fall apart tender. Serve immediately.

Slow Cooker Corned Beef Brisket with Cabbage

(Serves 6-8)

Corned beef brisket is a wonderful invention. You can eat it for dinner and then the next morning scramble eggs with it and have the most satisfying breakfast. Briskets are very forgiving cuts of meat, the key is to find one that's not pre-brined with chemical-filled liquids. You want a straight up brisket with a nice swath of fat on it, and then you want to salt the tarnation out of it.

3-4 pound brisket
Salt
1 tablespoon peppercorns
3 teaspoons minced garlic
1 onion, sliced
1 cup beef broth or chicken broth
1/2 head of cabbage, cut into 2" wedges

Season brisket liberally with salt. Place in a slow cooker, fatty side facing up. Pour over peppercorns, garlic, and onion slices. Pour broth around the side of brisket, season once more with salt. Cook on low for 6 hours, add cabbage wedges, cook 2-3 more hours or until cabbage and meat is tender.

Instant Pot Whole Roasted Chicken

(Yields 1 whole chicken)

I roast a chicken in the oven at least once a week, so why not change it up and use my Instant Pot? The Instant Pot is a great way to make a whole chicken without all the effort of basting, which requires, well, paying attention. Note that it's tricky to flip a whole chicken during the browning process as a whole chicken is unwieldy. Just make sure you have strong tongs or a large spatula. After you've cooked the bird, and you'd like to crisp back up the skin, you can fry the skin in a nonstick sauté pan on medium high heat on the stove.

1/4 cup salt
3-4 pound whole chicken, giblets removed and patted dry
2 sprigs fresh rosemary
3 lemon slices
1 teaspoon fresh minced rosemary leaves
1 teaspoon garlic powder
1/4 teaspoon smoked paprika
1 teaspoon plus 2 tablespoons olive oil, divided
1/2 cup chicken broth

Spread salt all over the outside and inside cavity of the chicken. Place in fridge 2-4 hours. Remove from fridge. Place rosemary sprigs and lemon slices inside cavity of chicken.

In a small mixing bowl, whisk together 1 teaspoon olive oil, minced rosemary leaves, garlic powder, and smoked paprika. Rub on chicken skin. Heat remaining two tablespoons olive oil in Instant Pot to Sauté setting on Hot. Brown both sides of chicken skin, at least 5-7 minutes per side, until skin is crispy, being very careful when turning chicken in the Instant Pot. Make sure the breast side of the chicken is facing up for the next step. Pour chicken broth around chicken, then cover with lid and make sure vent is set to "Sealing." Turn Instant Pot to Manual setting for 25 minutes. Let Manual cycle run its course, and let it depressurize naturally for 20 minutes, then flip the vent to "Venting" to allow the Instant Pot to depressurize. When the metal float valve has descended, it is safe to remove the lid. Remove chicken, slice and serve. Fry chicken skin in a nonstick sauté pan on medium high heat if desired.

Veggie Bolognese Lasagna

(Serves 10-12)

===

1 eggplant, sliced lengthwise into 1/4" thick slices
2 zucchini, thinly sliced lengthwise
1/2 butternut squash, softened in microwave for 3 minutes,
peeled and sliced into 1/4" thick slices

1 pound ground beef
1 teaspoon dried oregano
1 teaspoon salt
1/2 teaspoon onion powder
1/4 teaspoon garlic powder
1/4 teaspoon pepper

2 14-ounce cans of diced tomatoes
1/2 6-ounce can tomato paste
2 tablespoons olive oil, divided
1 teaspoon minced garlic (2-3 cloves)
10 basil leaves, chopped
1 teaspoon butter
Pinch of salt

2 cups milk
1/2 stick salted butter (4 tablespoons)
1/4 cup arrowroot powder
Pinch of nutmeg
1½ teaspoons salt
1/2 teaspoon pepper

1 ball fresh mozzerella - shredded, or 2 cups shredded mozzarella

===

Lay eggplant and zucchini slices out on paper towels. Season with salt. Let sweat 10-15 minutes, then dab them dry with paper towels.

In a large, flat sauté pan on medium high heat, brown meat with oregano, salt, onion powder, garlic powder, and pepper. Drain excess grease, set aside.

Make homemade marinara sauce. Pulse diced tomatoes and tomato paste in Vitamix or blender to purée. In a large saucepan, heat olive oil on medium heat until shimmering. Add garlic and basil, cook for 2 minutes, stirring.

Add in tomato purée and bring to a boil. Add in butter and a pinch of salt. Turn down heat to low and let simmer for 15-20 minutes, tasting and seasoning with additional salt if needed. Add browned meat to sauce and stir. Remove from heat.

Make béchamel sauce. Heat the milk in a saucepan on medium heat for about 3-4 minutes, until hot, being careful not to scald. Melt the butter in a saucepan on medium heat. Whisk in the arrowroot powder. Steadily pour in the heated milk, whisking constantly, making sure all clumps are whisked out. When milk mixture starts to boil, lower the heat, season with a pinch of salt, and let simmer gently. Whisk the mixture every 3-5 minutes. If béchamel sauce gets too thick, add in milk, 1 tablespoon at a time. Remove from heat. Add pinch of nutmeg, a twist or two of fresh pepper, and more salt if necessary.

Preheat oven to 400°. Roast zucchini and eggplant slices for 10 minutes on foil-lined baking sheets. Remove from oven and lay slices on a paper towel to let any excess water drain.

Grease a 10"x13" nonstick casserole dish with 1 tablespoon olive oil making sure entire bottom is covered. Place butternut squash slices on the bottom of the pan, season with salt and pepper. Bake in oven 10 minutes, remove from oven. Using a ladle, spread a thin layer of the meat sauce and then drizzle some béchamel sauce over the meat sauce. Place a layer of eggplant, season with salt and pepper. Repeat with a thin layer of the meat sauce and a thin layer of the béchamel. Next put the zucchini layer on top and season with salt and pepper. Drizzle one more thin layer béchamel over the zucchini, then spread the remaining amount of meat sauce over the béchamel. Top evenly with shredded mozzarella. Bake 30 minutes in oven, or until veggies are cooked through and cheese is starting to turn golden and bubbly.

CHICKEN, BROCCOLI, AND SWISS STOVETOP BAKE

(Serves 4-6)

1 tablespoon olive oil
1-2 pounds boneless skinless chicken thighs, cut into 1" pieces
Salt and pepper
8-ounce package button mushrooms, loosely chopped
1/2 onion, loosely chopped
1 teaspoon chopped fresh parsley leaves, plus more for garnish
2 cups broccoli florets
4 slices Swiss cheese

Heat olive oil to medium high heat in a large, flat-bottomed nonstick sauté pan. Add chicken thigh pieces, season liberally with salt and pepper. Cook for 2-3 minutes until chicken thighs start to brown. Add mushrooms, onion, and parsley, toss and sauté 5-7 more minutes, until chicken is cooked through and mushrooms are soft. Season with salt and pepper.

In a separate steamer pan, steam broccoli pieces until tender when pierced with a fork, about 8-10 minutes. Toss broccoli pieces in with chicken and mushrooms. Season once more with salt and pepper. Flatten out contents of pan and lay Swiss cheese slices evenly over top. Cover, turn heat down to low, and let simmer for 5-10 minutes until cheese is melted. Garnish with parsley and serve immediately.

Monterey Casserole

(Serves 6-8)

1 pound ground beef
1 small onion, chopped
1 green bell pepper, chopped
1 jalapeño, deseeded, destemmed,
and chopped
2 teaspoons minced garlic

1/2 tablespoon chili powder
1 teaspoon salt
1/2 teaspoon ground white pepper
1/2 teaspoon cumin
1/2 teaspoon onion powder

4 tablespoons butter
1/2 cup chicken broth
3/4 cup heavy cream
2 tablespoons sour cream
2 tablespoons cream cheese
1/2 teaspoon salt
1 4-ounce can fire roasted green chiles
1 tablespoon chopped fresh cilantro
leaves
2 cups shredded Monterey Jack
cheese, divided
Sour cream for serving

Preheat oven to 350°. In a sauté pan over medium high heat, brown ground beef and use spatula to chop into bite-sized pieces. After browned, let meat drain on a paper towel lined plate. Sauté onions, green bell pepper, jalapeño, and garlic in the same sauté pan with the meat drippings over medium high heat until soft, about 5-6 minutes. Add meat back into veggies and stir.

In a small bowl, whisk together chili powder, salt, white pepper, cumin, and onion powder. Sprinkle spice mix over meat and veggies, stirring to coat meat and veggies evenly. Remove from heat and pour into 8"x8" casserole pan.

In a large sauce pan, heat butter and chicken broth, add heavy cream, turn heat to low. Whisk in sour cream, cream cheese, and salt. Stir in green chiles, cilantro, and 1 cup of Monterey Jack cheese. Fold until melted. Pour on top of meat and veggies in casserole pan. Top with remaining cup of Monterey Jack cheese. Bake in oven 30 minutes or until golden and bubbling.

Jeannie's Seafood Stew

(Serves 8)

1/3 cup olive oil
1 fennel bulb, rough ends and top discarded, chopped
2 celery stalks, finely chopped
2 teaspoons minced garlic
1 sweet onion, minced
1 tablespoon dried oregano
1/8 teaspoon red pepper flakes
Salt and pepper
1 pound squid tubes, cut into 1/2" pieces
1 cup chicken broth
1 cup clam juice
1 tablespoon finely chopped lemon zest
1 tablespoon lemon juice
2 14-ounce cans diced tomatoes, one can puréed
2 tablespoons tomato paste
1 pound peeled, deveined shrimp
1 pound cod, halibut, haddock, or other whitefish, cut into 2" chunks
1/2 pound jumbo lump crab meat
1 pound black mussels, scrubbed clean
1/2 cup chopped flat leaf Italian parsley
1/4 cup freshly grated parmesan

In a large Dutch oven or Le Creuset pot, heat olive oil to medium high heat and add fennel, celery, garlic, onion, oregano, and red pepper flakes. Season liberally with salt and pepper. Let cook until veggies are soft, stirring occasionally, about 10-15 minutes. Turn heat to medium low and add squid, cook 8-10 minutes, stirring occasionally. Pour in the chicken broth, clam juice, lemon zest, and lemon juice. Season with salt and pepper, bring to a boil. Add in tomatoes and tomato paste, season once again with salt and pepper. Bring to boil again. Add shrimp and let cook 2-3 minutes until shrimp is cooked through. Add fish pieces and crab, let cook another 2-3 minutes. Stir in mussels, cover, and let cook 4-5 minutes, until mussel shells open. Remove lid, season once more with salt and pepper. Serve in large bowls garnished with chopped parsley and grated parmesan.

Watermelon Gazpacho

(Serves 4)

Traditional gazpacho can be too acidic, so I added watermelon for brightness, smoothness, and some good old fashioned summer sweet. This recipe will test your knife skills, so get a good one and sharpen it.

1 14-ounce can diced tomatoes, puréed
2 cups watermelon chunks, puréed
3 green onions, white and palest green parts chopped
1 cup diced cherry tomatoes
1 cup finely diced red pepper
1 cup finely diced English cucumber
1/4 cup diced red onion
1 tablespoon minced parsley
1 teaspoon minced garlic
1 tablespoon white wine vinegar
1 teaspoon cumin
1/2 teaspoon salt
1/4 teaspoon fresh pepper
1/8 teaspoon ground cayenne

Combine all ingredients in a large mixing bowl, stirring well. Chill in fridge for 2-4 hours to let the flavors marry, then serve chilled.

CREAMY CHICKEN SOUP

(Serves 6-8)

1-2 pounds boneless chicken thighs, cut into 1/2" pieces
Salt and pepper
1 tablespoon olive oil
1 cup chopped carrots
1½ cups chopped leeks, white and pale green parts only
1 tablespoon white wine vinegar
6 cups chicken broth
2-3 sprigs fresh thyme or 1/2 teaspoon dried thyme
3/4 cup heavy cream (use coconut cream for dairy free)
2 tablespoons chopped chives, for garnish

Season chicken thighs with salt and pepper. In a large Dutch oven or Le Creuset, heat olive oil to medium high heat. Sauté chicken thighs 7-8 minutes, then remove from pot, leaving pan drippings. Add carrots, scraping bottom of pan to remove any drippings from the chicken pieces, let cook 1-2 minutes. Add chopped leeks, letting cook an additional 2-3 minutes, letting the leeks get a little browned, but not burned. Sprinkle in white wine vinegar, let cook 1-2 more minutes. Pour in chicken broth and add thyme sprigs. Bring to boil and let cook 8-10 minutes on a rolling boil. Reduce heat to medium low and add back in chicken pieces. Let cook 3-4 minutes, then add heavy cream and cook 1-2 more minutes. Discard thyme sprigs and serve soup immediately, garnished with chopped chives.

Instant Pot Beef Pho

(Serves 4-6)

Pho is a Vietnamese beef bone broth soup usually made with bun noodles (rice vermicelli). My version loses the sugar (sorry, no hoisin sauce) and the starchy rice noodles, but keeps the flavor and adds zucchini noodles for maximum pho-lavor. I will not apologize for that last pun, nor will I apologize for how much you will love this soup.

---

1 tablespoon olive oil

1 onion, thinly sliced

2 teaspoons minced garlic

2 1" fresh ginger pieces, peeled (or use 1/2 teaspoon ground ginger)

4 teaspoons salt, divided

1/2 teaspoon fresh ground pepper

8 cups water

2 pounds beef bones

1 tablespoon gluten free soy sauce or coconut aminos

1 tablespoon fish sauce

3 anise pods (also called star anise)

1 cinnamon stick

2 boneless rib-eye steaks, frozen for 3-4 hours

2 zucchini, spiralized into noodles, salted and patted dry

1 cup bean sprouts, for garnish

Thai basil leaves (or regular basil) for garnish

1 tablespoon cilantro leaves for garnish

Mint leaves for garnish

2 jalapeños, sliced for garnish

Sriracha for garnish

Place Instant Pot on Sauté setting. Heat olive oil to shimmering and sauté onion slices, garlic, and ginger. Add 2 teaspoons salt and 1/2 teaspoon pepper and cook until soft, about 3-4 minutes. Add water, beef bones, soy sauce, fish sauce, anise pods, cinnamon stick, and remaining 2 teaspoons salt. Cover Instant Pot, with the vent set to "Sealing" and switch to Manual setting at 30 minutes.

Let Instant Pot pressure cook its natural cycle until the float valve descends naturally and you can safely remove the lid. Remove bones, anise pods, and cinnamon stick from broth. Skim off and discard excess fat from top of broth if necessary. Switch Instant Pot back to Sauté setting and bring soup to a slight boil.

Remove steaks from freezer and slice as thinly as possible. Season steak slices with additional salt and pepper. When soup is boiling, gently drop steak slices into soup. As steak cooks in boiling soup, skim off any excess foam. Pat dry zucchini noodles one last time, and drop into soup. Let cook 3-4 minutes, then turn off Instant Pot. Serve soup immediately, garnished with bean sprouts, basil leaves, mint leaves, sliced jalapeño, and a smattering of Sriracha.

Avgolemono Soup

(Serves 6-8)

8 cups chicken broth
10-12 ounces frozen or fresh cauliflower rice
or 1 head cauliflower, grated into rice
3 eggs
2 tablespoons lemon juice (about 2 lemons)
2 cups pulled and chopped rotisserie chicken
Salt and pepper
Parsley, chopped for garnish
Lemon slices for garnish

Heat up chicken broth on medium high heat in large soup pot. Add cauliflower rice and season with salt and pepper. Bring to a boil, reduce heat to low, cook for 3-5 minutes. Add 1 teaspoon salt and 1/2 teaspoon pepper.

In a bowl, whisk together the lemon juice and eggs until pale yellow, about 20-30 seconds. Ladle 1 cup of hot broth into bowl of lemon-egg and whisk together until mixed.

Slowly pour the broth-lemon-egg mixture back into soup pot, stirring soup with wooden spoon. The soup will thicken and turn creamy as the egg cooks. Add in chicken, season one more time with salt and pepper to taste.

Serve immediately and garnish with parsley and lemon slices.

BROCCOLI CHEDDAR SOUP

(Serves 6-8)

2 tablespoons butter
1 medium onion, chopped
16 ounces broccoli florets, chopped to 1/4" pieces
2 tablespoons white wine vinegar
4 cups chicken broth
1/2 tablespoon onion powder
1/2 tablespoon garlic powder
Salt and pepper
2 tablespoons arrowroot powder
4 cups grated medium cheddar, plus extra for garnish

Heat butter on medium high heat in a large Dutch oven or Le Creuset. Sauté chopped onion until soft, about 7-9 minutes. Add broccoli pieces and toss with onions, let cook for 2-3 minutes. Stir in white wine vinegar. Add chicken broth, then stir in onion powder and garlic powder, season liberally with salt and pepper. Whisk in arrowroot powder, 1 tablespoon at a time until fully mixed. Bring to a boil, then reduce heat and let simmer 8-10 minutes until broccoli is cooked and tender. Add in grated cheddar, stirring until melted. Season once more with salt and pepper to taste, and serve with extra grated cheddar for garnish.

Roasted Tomato Basil Soup

(Serves 6-8)

1 pint cherry tomatoes
10 heirloom tomatoes, tops and excess seeds removed, cut into 2" chunks
4 tablespoons olive oil, divided
Salt and pepper
1 onion, diced
1 teaspoon celery salt
1 teaspoon garlic powder
2 teaspoons salt
1/2 teaspoon ground white pepper
2 cups packed basil leaves, chopped
2 cups chicken broth (use veggie broth for vegetarian)
1 cup heavy cream (use coconut cream for dairy free)

Preheat oven to 400°. In a large bowl, toss cherry tomatoes and heirloom tomato chunks with 3 tablespoons olive oil. Season with salt and pepper. Roast in the oven for 30 minutes, until tomatoes are blistered and soft.

Meanwhile, in a large Dutch oven or Le Creuset, heat remaining tablespoon of olive oil to medium high heat. Sauté onions until soft, about 3-4 minutes. Add celery salt, garlic powder, salt, and white pepper and cook 2 minutes. Add in cooked tomatoes, basil leaves, and chicken broth, bring to boil, then reduce heat and let simmer for 15-20 minutes. Turn off heat and purée in batches in a Vitamix or strong blender until smooth. Pour soup back into Le Creuset and whisk in heavy cream until smooth. Season with salt and pepper if necessary. Serve immediately.

MISO BACON SOUP

(Serves 6)

6 cups water
1/3 cup miso paste
1 teaspoon salt
1/2 teaspoon pepper
2 cups button mushrooms, thinly sliced
1 cup diced snap peas
1 baby bok choy, hard end discarded, thinly chopped
3 green onions, palest white part thinly sliced (about 1/4 cup)
6 slices bacon, cooked crispy and chopped
Small toasted nori papers, cut into 3" pieces (about 1/2 cup)

Heat 5 cups of water in a large sauce pan over medium high heat. Place miso paste in strong blender with remaining cup of water and pulse until dissolved, about 20-30 seconds. Pour into sauce pan. Bring to a boil, add salt and pepper. Add mushrooms, snap peas, baby bok choy, green onions, and bacon pieces. Let simmer 5-7 minutes. Add nori papers, stir, season once more with salt and pepper, serve.

SIDES

Low Carb Fried Green Tomatoes ... 131

Glazed Portobello Mushrooms ... 132

Portobello Cap with Zhoug ... 133

Sesame Baby Bok Choy ... 135

Green Beans with
Creamy Horseradish Dill ... 136

Roasted Brussels Sprouts with Balsamic
and Goat Cheese Crumbles ... 137

Minted Brussels Sprouts with
Blistered Cherry Tomatoes ... 138

Chopped Asparagus with
Shallots and Cream ... 139

Chard Asparagus Casserole ... 141

Asparagus with Prosciutto Crumbles ... 142

Coconut Lime Broccoli ... 144

Broccoli Fritters ... 145

Stuffed Pasilla Peppers ...147

Yellow Squash Casserole ... 148

Roasted Zucchini & Squash Tian ... 151

Lemongrass Thyme Cauliflower
"Steaks" ... 152

Green Chile Cauliflower
"Rice" Casserole ... 153

Green Bean Tomato Butter Lettuce Salad
with Lemon Chive Dressing ... 154

Cucumber and Green Apple Slaw ... 155

Veggie Salad ...156

Lemon Dijon Tahini Dressing ... 157

Cilantro Green Goddess Dressing ... 157

Grilled Peach and Burrata Salad ... 158

Cucumber Tomato Avocado
Side Salad ... 160

Roasted Eggplant, Goat Cheese,
and Basil Terrine ... 162

Zucchini Noodles and Salmon with
Lemon Garlic Cream Sauce ... 163

Zucchini Roll Ups ... 165

Zucchini Noodles Alfredo ... 167

Green Curry Sweet Potato Noodles
with Eggplant ... 168

Savory Mashed Sweet Potatoes ... 170

Parsnip Purée ... 171

Butternut Squash Fries with
Spicy Ranch Dressing ... 172

LOW CARB FRIED GREEN TOMATOES

(Serves 4)

4 large green unripe heirloom tomatoes
1/2 cup coconut flour
2 eggs
2 tablespoons whole milk or coconut milk
1 cup almond flour
1 teaspoon salt
1/4 teaspoon freshly ground pepper
1/2 teaspoon onion powder
3/4 cup olive oil, coconut oil, or beef tallow for frying

Slice tomatoes into 1/2" slices, discarding ends. In a shallow bowl, spread out coconut flour. In a second shallow bowl, beat eggs and milk with a fork. In a third shallow bowl, whisk together almond flour, salt, pepper, and onion powder.

Pour oil into a cast iron skillet and heat oil until hot enough that when you drop a sprinkle of almond flour into the oil, it sizzles. Coat one tomato slice in coconut flour, then dredge in egg/milk mixture, then coat with almond flour. Immediately place into cast iron pan, and quickly repeat with two more tomato slices. While tomato slices cook on the first side, rinse your hands as they will become very sticky with the batter. After cooking 2-3 minutes, being mindful not to burn the almond flour coating, flip the tomato slices and cook the other side for an additional 1-2 minutes. Place the three slices on a paper towel lined plate to drain, and repeat the process, three more tomato slices at a time until all are cooked. Serve hot.

Glazed Portobello Mushrooms

(Serves 3-4)

2 pounds portobello or baby bella mushrooms, cut into 1½" pieces
4 tablespoons olive oil, divided
Salt and pepper
1 teaspoon fresh or dried thyme leaves
1 teaspoon fresh or dried oregano leaves
1/2 teaspoon fresh ground pepper
1/2 cup balsamic vinegar
1½ teaspoons minced garlic

Preheat oven to 400°. In a large sauté pan, heat 2 tablespoons of olive oil on medium high heat. Lay mushroom pieces evenly in pan, season with salt and pepper. Cook until mushrooms are browning and shrinking, about 10 minutes, stirring every few minutes to make sure the mushrooms are cooking evenly on all sides. Remove mushrooms from heat.

In a mixing bowl, whisk together 2 remaining tablespoons of olive oil, the thyme and oregano leaves, fresh ground pepper, balsamic vinegar, and minced garlic. Pour mushroom pieces from pan into liquid and mix to make sure mushrooms are evenly coated. Spread coated mushroom pieces evenly onto a foil-lined baking sheet.

Roast in oven for 20 minutes, checking to make sure mushrooms do not burn. Flip mushrooms halfway through cooking time. Remove from oven and season with salt once more before serving.

Portobello Cap with Zhoug

(Serves 4)

2 tablespoons olive oil
4 portobello mushroom caps
Salt and pepper
1/2 cup sun-dried tomato paste (or 1/2 cup sun dried tomatoes,
puréed in a blender)
Fresh ball of mozzarella, sliced into 1/2" disks
Zhoug (p. 223)

In a large, flat-bottomed sauté pan, heat olive oil to medium high heat. Season portobello caps with salt and pepper, then cook until softened and browned, about 10-15 minutes, flipping halfway through cooking. Remove from heat and set caps on a paper towel to let drain.

Preheat oven broiler to low setting. Lay portobello caps on a foil-lined baking sheet. Spread sun dried tomato paste evenly atop caps, then press one slice of mozzarella into each cap. Place on top shelf of oven and broil 4-5 minutes, until cheese is bubbly and brown, making sure it doesn't burn. Remove from oven and let stand 5-10 minutes. Serve, garnished along the top with Zhoug (p. 223).

SESAME BABY BOK CHOY

(Serves 2-3)

═══════════════════════════════

4 heads baby bok choy, ends trimmed, washed
2 tablespoons olive oil
1/2 teaspoon sesame oil
1/2 onion, thinly sliced
2 stalks celery, thinly sliced
1 tablespoon miso paste
1 tablespoon water
Salt and pepper
1 teaspoon sesame seeds, for garnish

═══════════════════════════════

Cut off and discard bottom flat ends of baby bok choy. Heat olive oil and sesame oil to medium high heat in a large sauté pan, and cook onion and celery until soft, about 3-4 minutes. Add in miso paste and use a rubber spatula to spread it around the onions and celery. Sprinkle water to help dilute the miso paste. Season with salt and pepper. Add bok choy pieces and toss with miso covered onions and celery. Cook 2 minutes. Cover and turn heat to low for 4-5 minutes until bok choy is soft. Remove from heat, season with salt and pepper, toss once more, and serve garnished with sesame seeds.

GREEN BEANS WITH CREAMY HORSERADISH DILL

(Serves 4-6)

2 pounds green beans
3 tablespoons plus 1 teaspoon olive oil, divided
1 teaspoon salt
1/2 teaspoon pepper
1/2 teaspoon onion powder
1/2 teaspoon garlic powder
1/2 cup sour cream
1 tablespoon prepared horseradish
1 tablespoon minced dill
1 teaspoon lemon juice
1/2 teaspoon minced lemon zest, plus more for garnish
1 tablespoon water
1/2 cup chopped hazelnuts (or preferred nut)

Preheat oven to 400°. In a large plastic bag, shake green beans, 3 tablespoons olive oil, salt, pepper, onion powder, and garlic powder until green beans are coated in oil and seasoning. Line a baking sheet with parchment paper and pour green beans evenly onto baking sheet. Bake 10 minutes, stir green beans, bake 10 more minutes until done and starting to char.

In a small mixing bowl, whisk together sour cream, horseradish, dill, lemon juice, and lemon zest. Stir in 1 tablespoon water to thin out the sauce. Toss green beans with creamy horseradish dill sauce.

Heat remaining teaspoon of olive oil in a small nonstick pan to medium high heat. Toast hazelnut pieces until golden brown, but not burned. Garnish green beans with toasted hazelnuts and lemon zest.

Roasted Brussels Sprouts with Balsamic and Goat Cheese Crumbles

(Serves 8)

===

2 pounds Brussels sprouts
1/4 cup olive oil
1/4 cup balsamic vinegar, plus more for drizzling
1 teaspoon garlic powder
Salt and pepper
1/2 cup goat cheese

===

Preheat oven to 375°. Cut bottoms off of Brussels sprouts and discard. Quarter remaining sprouts and use your hands to separate the easily removable leaves. Place leaves into a large mixing bowl. Chop remaining sprouts centers to 1/4" pieces, then add to the mixing bowl.

In a smaller bowl, whisk together olive oil, vinegar, and garlic powder. Drizzle onto sprouts, and use your hands to toss to make sure the sprouts are coated. Pour sprouts onto two nonstick foil-lined baking sheets. Roast in oven 30-40 minutes, stirring sprouts every 10-15 minutes so the leaves don't burn. In last remaining 5 minutes of cooking, sprinkle goat cheese using your hand to drop it in little pieces evenly over baking sheet, toss with sprouts. Remove from oven and season again with salt and pepper, drizzle with extra balsamic if desired, and serve.

MINTED BRUSSELS SPROUTS WITH BLISTERED CHERRY TOMATOES

(Serves 4-6)

3 tablespoons chopped walnuts
1 pint cherry tomatoes
Salt and pepper
2 tablespoons olive oil, divided
1 shallot, minced
1 pound Brussels sprouts, bottoms cut and discarded, cut lengthwise into disks
2 tablespoons white wine vinegar
1/2 cup peas
1 tablespoon chopped mint leaves, plus additional for garnish

Preheat oven to 400°. Spread walnuts evenly on baking sheet, roast for 8-10 minutes, being careful not to burn. Remove from oven, set walnuts aside in a bowl, wipe off baking sheet.

Spread cherry tomatoes evenly on baking sheet, drizzle with 1 tablespoon of olive oil, season with salt and pepper. Roast in oven for 20 minutes, or until tomato skin is breaking and blistered.

Heat 1 remaining tablespoon of olive oil in a large sauté pan on medium high heat. Cook shallot until soft, about 3-4 minutes. Add in Brussels sprouts, tossing to coat in oil and shallots. Drizzle in white wine vinegar and season with salt and pepper. Let sautée about 5-7 minutes until starting to soften. Fold in peas, let cook additional 1-2 minutes. Turn off heat and add in toasted walnuts, blistered cherry tomatoes, and mint. Season once more with salt and pepper and mix all ingredients well, being careful not to smash the cherry tomatoes. Serve immediately with additional mint for garnish.

Chopped Asparagus with Shallots and Cream

(Serves 4)

1 shallot, minced
2 tablespoons butter
1 pound asparagus, rough ends trimmed and discarded,
then cut into 1/2" pieces
1/4 cup chicken broth
1 teaspoon salt
1/4 cup heavy cream
Freshly ground pepper, for seasoning

Heat butter in a nonstick sauté pan on medium high heat until melted and bubbling. Cook shallots until soft, about 3 minutes. Add asparagus pieces, chicken broth, and salt. Cook for 3-4 minutes, until asparagus is green and tender. Remove from heat. Stir in heavy cream, season with salt and pepper to taste, serve.

CHARD ASPARAGUS CASSEROLE

(Serves 6-8)

====================

1 pound rainbow chard, cleaned thoroughly, rough ends trimmed and discarded
1 pound asparagus, rough ends trimmed and discarded
Salt and pepper
3 tablespoons butter, divided
1/2 cup heavy cream
1/4 teaspoon celery salt
1/8 teaspoon ground cayenne
1½ cups freshly grated parmesan

====================

Cut the center stems of the chard away from the leaves. Loosely chop the leaves and set them aside. Chop the stems into 1/2" pieces. Chop the asparagus into 1/2" pieces. In a large pot of boiling water, boil the chard stems until they are soft and tender to pierce with a fork, about 3-4 minutes. Remove from water and place on a towel to dry. Boil the asparagus pieces for 2-3 minutes, remove from water and place on a towel to dry. Boil the chopped chard leaves for 2-3 minutes, remove from water and place on a towel to dry.

Preheat oven to 400°. Grease a 9 x 12 casserole dish with 1 tablespoon of the butter. Sprinkle a layer of salt over the butter. Spread the chard leaves over the butter. Season with salt and pepper. Sprinkle the asparagus pieces over the chard leaves. Season with salt and pepper. Sprinkle the chard stem pieces and season with salt and pepper. In a small bowl, whisk together the heavy cream, celery salt, and ground cayenne. Drizzle the cream over the vegetables. Top evenly with the grated parmesan. Cube the remaining two tablespoons of butter, and place them spaced out evenly over the parmesan. Bake in oven for 20 minutes, until parmesan starts to brown and crisp. Remove from oven, let stand 5-10 minutes, then serve immediately.

ASPARAGUS WITH PROSCIUTTO CRUMBLES

(Serves 4)

1 pound asparagus, rough ends trimmed and discarded
Salt and pepper
1 tablespoon olive oil
1 tablespoon minced shallot
3 ounces prosciutto (about 5-6 slices), chopped
1/4 cup almond flour
3/4 cup heavy cream
1/2 cup grated parmesan

Place asparagus in an 8"x8" baking dish. Season well with salt and pepper. Pour heavy cream evenly over asparagus.

Preheat oven to 400°. Heat olive oil to medium high heat in a large nonstick pan. Cook shallot until soft, about 2 minutes. Add prosciutto pieces, stirring to fry them up evenly until they are crispy. Stir in almond flour until "crumbles" form and cook an additional 3-4 minutes until it starts to become golden brown.

Pour prosciutto crumbles evenly over asparagus. Roast in oven for 10 minutes. Remove from oven and sprinkle parmesan on top. Place back in oven and bake an additional 10 minutes or until parmesan starts to turn golden. Serve immediately.

Coconut Lime Broccoli

(Serves 4-5)

---

1 tablespoon olive oil
1 shallot, minced
Salt and pepper
1 tablespoon grated fresh ginger
1 teaspoon coconut aminos or gluten free soy sauce
1 can full-fat coconut cream or milk, clear liquid discarded
(check for no sugar on label)
Juice of half a lime
2 broccoli crowns, cut into small florets
1/4 cup chopped cilantro leaves

Heat olive oil to medium high heat in nonstick sauce pan. Add shallots and cook 3-4 minutes, season with salt and pepper. Stir in ginger and coconut aminos and cook an additional 2-3 minutes. Add in coconut milk and lime juice. Stir as the mixture comes to a boil. Add in broccoli florets and toss in sauce making sure all the broccoli is coated. Cover, reduce heat to low, and steam for 5 minutes until broccoli is bright green and tender. Toss broccoli again in sauce and garnish with a squeeze of lime and fresh cilantro.

Broccoli Fritters

(Yields 10-12 fritters)

1 pound broccoli florets, cut into 1/8"-1/4" pieces
2 tablespoons chopped green onion
1/2 cup shredded Colby Jack cheese
1 teaspoon xanthan gum or arrowroot powder
2 eggs, beaten
1/2 cup almond flour
1 teaspoon salt
1/2 teaspoon fresh pepper
3 tablespoons olive oil

In a large mixing bowl, combine all ingredients, except for the olive oil. Mix well and form mixture into 2" wide x 1" high disks.

Heat olive oil in a large, flat sauté pan to medium high heat. Do a sizzle test by dropping a pinch of the mixture into the oil. Once it sizzles, the oil is ready to fry.

Place disks onto hot oil, gently press each disk flatter with a spatula, being careful that disks don't stick to the back of the spatula. Cook 2-3 minutes until browned, then gingerly flip disks and smash flatter with spatula again. Cook additional 2-3 minutes until browned but not burned. Transfer to paper towel to drain excess oil and serve immediately.

Stuffed Pasilla Peppers

(Serves 2-4)

2 large pasilla or poblano peppers, or 3-4 smaller ones
1 tablespoon olive oil
1/3 cup green onions, white and pale green parts, chopped
1 teaspoon dried oregano
1 cup grated sharp white cheddar cheese
1/4 cup Cotija cheese, crumbled
1/4 cup grated pepper Jack cheese (optional, for a kick)
1/2 cup pre-cooked shrimp, loosely chopped
Cilantro, chopped for garnish
Salsa for garnish

Hold peppers over open flame on stove or grill until the skin blisters. Remove from heat and let cool. Peel skin off all peppers and discard. Carefully cut a lengthwise slit into pepper, cutting out and discarding seeds and veins inside. Lay peppers in an 8"x8" baking dish.

Preheat oven to 350°. In a nonstick sauté pan, heat olive oil to medium high heat. Cook green onions and oregano until soft, about 3-4 minutes, stirring so as not to burn the green onions. Turn off heat and add cheese and shrimp. Toss around with onions until mixed, but not entirely melted. Scoop cheese mixture evenly into prepared peppers in baking dish. Bake in oven 15 minutes until cheese is melted well. Serve immediately, topped with cilantro and a dollop of salsa

Yellow Squash Casserole

(Serves 4-6)

3-4 yellow squash, cut into 1/2" pieces
Salt and pepper
2 eggs
3/4 cup heavy cream
2 cups shredded Colby Jack cheese, divided
1 red pepper, diced
4 slices bacon
1½ cups almond flour
1 tablespoon butter, plus more to grease the baking dish

Lay squash pieces out on kitchen towels. Season with salt and let "sweat" for 15-20 minutes. Using paper towels, press excess water out of squash pieces. Preheat oven to 400°. Grease a 9"x12" or 10"x13" baking dish with butter. Pour in squash pieces, season with salt and pepper.

In a small mixing bowl, whisk together eggs and heavy cream. Season with salt and pepper. Whisk in 1 cup of the shredded Colby Jack and all the diced pepper. Pour over squash pieces, toss with hands until squash is coated with cheese and pepper mixture. Season once more with salt and pepper. Bake in oven for 20 minutes.

Heat a large, flat-bottomed sauté pan to medium high heat and cook bacon pieces until crispy, about 8-10 minutes. Remove bacon pieces and let drain on a paper towel, reserving bacon drippings in pan. Add in almond flour and butter into pan, season with salt and pepper, and toast the almond flour until fragrant and starting to turn golden, about 3-minutes. Break bacon slices into bits, and stir into almond flour. Pour almond flour into a mixing bowl, add 1/2 cup shredded Colby Jack, then pour onto squash casserole and toss with squash mixture. Top with remaining 1/2 cup shredded Colby Jack cheese. Put back into oven for 10 minutes, or until top is golden and bubbly.

ROASTED ZUCCHINI & SQUASH TIAN

(Serves 2-4)

Based on a classic French dish, this casserole is deceptively simple yet overwhelming in flavor. I recommend doubling the recipe, or even stacking two layers of zucchini and squash, making sure to season each layer with salt, pepper, and thyme leaves.

=====

1 tablespoon olive oil, plus more for drizzling
2 leeks, white and palest green parts only, chopped
5-7 basil leaves, chopped
Salt and pepper
2 zucchini, sliced into disks
2 yellow squash, sliced into disks
1 teaspoon fresh thyme leaves

=====

Preheat oven to 425°.

Heat the olive oil in a sauté pan on medium high heat. Sauté leeks and basil until soft, being careful not to burn, about 3-4 minutes. Season with salt and pepper. Remove from heat and pour into a 9"x12" baking dish, spreading evenly. Place zucchini and squash disks into baking dish in a scalloped pattern, overlapping and alternating colors per row. Season with salt and pepper, drizzle with olive oil, and sprinkle with thyme leaves. Bake for 25-30 minutes, or until zucchini and squash look softened and shrunk and have browned on the edges.

Lemongrass Thyme Cauliflower "Steaks"

(Serves 2-4)

---

4 tablespoons fresh squeezed lemon juice
4 tablespoons fresh squeezed orange juice
4 tablespoons olive oil
2 tablespoons Dijon mustard
4 teaspoons lemongrass paste (available in produce section of grocery store)
Salt and pepper
1 head of cauliflower
Coconut oil spray for baking sheet
6-8 thyme sprigs

Cut the center part of cauliflower head lengthwise into 2-4 1" thick "steaks." Preheat oven to 450°. In a mixing bowl, whisk together lemon juice, orange juice, olive oil, Dijon mustard, and lemongrass paste. Season with salt and pepper to taste. Lay cauliflower "steaks" in a flat dish and pour marinade over them, gently dredging with marinade to cover them completely. Spray a nonstick foil-lined baking sheet with coconut oil. Lay cauliflower "steaks" flat on baking sheet. Pour remaining marinade into a small sauce pan. Bake cauliflower 8 minutes, remove from oven and spread thyme sprigs around cauliflower. Place back in oven and cook 10 more minutes. Meanwhile, bring remaining marinade in saucepan to a boil, reduce heat and let simmer while cauliflower roasts. Remove cauliflower "steaks" from oven, flip them over, season once more with salt and pepper and bake 5 more minutes. Serve, drizzled with reduced marinade.

Green Chile Cauliflower "Rice" Casserole

(Serves 2-3)

If you, like me, try to avoid dairy, you can certainly make this dish and enjoy it every bit as much as our dairy-eating brethren. All you have to do is substitute dairy free cream cheese, or make your own by soaking 1/4 cup cashews for 8-12 hours in water, then purée it in a blender. Then sub dairy free cheddar for the regular cheese. Boom. Dairy free and delicious.

---

1 tablespoon olive oil
1/2 medium onion, chopped
1 4-ounce can fire-roasted, diced green chiles, drained of excess juices
1 12 or 16-ounce bag pre-cut cauliflower "rice,"
or 1 head of cauliflower, grated into rice
2 tablespoons cream cheese
Salt and pepper
1/2 cup grated sharp cheddar, divided
Cilantro, chopped, for garnish

Preheat oven to 350°. Heat olive oil in a large sauté pan on medium high heat, cook onion until soft, about 4-5 minutes. Add in green chiles, cauliflower "rice," salt, and pepper and sauté for 4-5 minutes until soft. Spoon in cream cheese and blend in. Stir in 1/4 cup of the grated cheddar, then remove from heat and pour contents into a small casserole dish or larger ramekin. Sprinkle remaining 1/4 cup grated cheddar on top. Bake for 10 minutes, until cheese is melted. Garnish with cilantro and serve.

Green Bean Tomato Butter Lettuce Salad with Lemon Chive Dressing

(Serves 4)

1 pound green beans, ends trimmed and discarded, cut into 1-inch pieces
Juice of half a lemon
1 tablespoon chives, chopped
1/2 cup mayonnaise (check the label for no sugar)
1 teaspoon Dijon mustard
Salt and pepper
2 heads butter lettuce, bottom stem discarded,
leaves torn into salad sized pieces
1 pint cherry tomatoes, halved

In a large saucepan, boil 4 cups of water on high heat. Blanch the green bean pieces by dropping them in the water for 4-5 minutes or until tender and bright green. Drain the beans, rinse them in cold water, and wrap in a clean kitchen towel to dry them. Store in fridge for 10 minutes to cool.

In a mixing bowl, whisk together lemon juice, chives, mayonnaise, Dijon mustard, salt, and pepper into a dressing. In a large salad bowl, toss the butter lettuce leaves, cherry tomatoes, and green bean pieces with the dressing and serve.

Cucumber and Green Apple Slaw

(Serves 8)

3 granny smith apples, cored and chopped into matchsticks
3 large seedless cucumbers, spiralized,
then chopped into smaller 2-3" pieces
Juice of half a lemon
1/4 cup olive oil
1/4 cup mayonnaise
1 tablespoon white wine vinegar
1 teaspoon salt
1/2 teaspoon fresh pepper
1 tablespoon finely chopped chives

In a large salad bowl, combine apple and cucumber pieces. In a small mixing bowl, whisk together lemon juice, olive oil, mayonnaise, white wine vinegar, salt, pepper, and chives into a dressing. Pour dressing over apple and cucumber and gently toss until coated. Place in fridge at least 1 hour before serving.

VEGGIE SALAD

(serves 2)

This is the freshest, brightest spring salad you'll ever need. Top with Lemon Tahini Dressing or Green Goddess Dressing.

---

3 tablespoons pumpkin seeds
Salt
1/2 pound asparagus, rough ends trimmed and discarded,
chopped into 1" pieces
1 cup cherry tomatoes, quartered
1 english cucumber, sliced
1-2 watermelon radishes, ends discarded, thinly sliced and quartered
8-10 pitted black olives, sliced

Heat a small nonstick pan to medium heat and toast pumpkin seeds, seasoning with salt, until starting to become brown and fragrant, about 3-4 minutes, tossing often.

Heat water in a small sauce pan to boiling, season water with a pinch of salt. Blanch asparagus pieces for 2-3 minutes until they turn bright green, drain immediately and let cool, season with salt.

In large mixing bowl, toss toasted pumpkin seeds, asparagus pieces, cherry tomatoes, watermelon radish slices, and olives. Dress with Lemon Tahini Dressing or Green Goddess Dressing. Serve.

Lemon Dijon Tahini Dressing

(Yields 3/4 cup)

1/4 cup tahini
1/4 cup water
Juice of half a lemon
1 tablespoon Dijon mustard
Smoked paprika, for garnish

Combine tahini, water, lemon juice, and Dijon mustard in a food processor or strong blender. Add more water if dressing is too thick. Garnish with a sprinkle of smoked paprika, if desired.

Cilantro Green Goddess Dressing

(Yields 1 cup)

1/3 cup crème fraîche, or use full fat canned coconut milk for dairy free
1 large avocado, peeled and pitted
Juice of half a lemon
1/2 teaspoon minced garlic
1 teaspoon Dijon mustard
3 tablespoons chopped fresh chives
3 tablespoons chopped cilantro leaves (or you can use Italian parsley leaves)
1 tablespoon chopped tarragon
1/2 teaspoon salt
1/2 teaspoon freshly ground pepper
1-2 tablespoons water, for thinning the dressing

Combine all ingredients in a food processor or strong blender. Add more or less water depending on desired consistency.

GRILLED PEACH AND BURRATA SALAD

(Serves 4)

2 peaches sliced in half, pit discarded
4 cups of arugula
Half an English cucumber, sliced
2 balls fresh burrata separated into 4 servings
2 avocados, halved, pitted, and chopped into chunks

DRESSING

6 tablespoons olive oil
2 tablespoons balsamic vinegar
1 teaspoon salt
1/2 teaspoon pepper
1 teaspoon fresh thyme leaves

Heat up a nonstick grill pan to medium high heat and grill peach halves until starting to soften, about 2 minutes. Remove from heat. Split arugula into four serving dishes. Top arugula with grilled peaches, cucumber, burrata, and avocado. In a mixing bowl, whisk together all dressing ingredients. Drizzle evenly over salad dishes and serve immediately while peach halves are still warm.

Cucumber Tomato Avocado Side Salad

(Serves 4)

1 English cucumber, diced
1 cup diced cherry tomatoes
1/2 cup diced red onion
1/2 teaspoon salt
1/4 teaspoon garlic powder
1/4 teaspoon onion powder
1 tablespoon chopped fresh parsley leaves
2 avocados, peeled and pitted, then chopped

Dressing

3 tablespoons olive oil
1 tablespoon lemon juice
1 tablespoon balsamic vinegar
1/2 tablespoon red wine vinegar
Salt and pepper

Combine all salad ingredients in a large mixing bowl. In a smaller bowl whisk dressing ingredients together, pour and toss with salad until coated. Serve immediately.

Roasted Eggplant, Goat Cheese, and Basil Terrine
(Serves 6-8)

2 eggplants, cut into 1/2" slices
Salt and pepper
1 cup packed fresh basil leaves
3 tablespoons olive oil, divided, plus more for drizzling
1/2 cup goat cheese
2 tablespoons cream cheese
2 tablespoons sour cream or crème fraîche
12-ounce jar roasted red peppers, drained and dried

Preheat oven to 400°. Lay eggplant slices on baking sheets, season with salt. Let stand for 10-15 minutes while eggplants "sweat." Dab off excess water with a paper towel, season with additional salt and pepper, and roast in oven 15 minutes. Flip eggplant pieces and cook for an additional 15 minutes, until eggplants are cooked through and soft and tender. Remove from oven, let cool, and cut off eggplant skins.

In a food processor or strong blender, combine basil leaves, 2 tablespoons olive oil, and additional salt and pepper. Blend until pulverized into a smooth pesto.

In a small mixing bowl, combine goat cheese, cream cheese, and sour cream.

Grease the sides of an an 8x4 loaf pan with remaining tablespoon of olive oil, arrange a layer of eggplant, then crumble some of the cheese mixture, then roasted peppers, then basil mixture, one after the other, ending with a layer of eggplant. Press everything firmly into the pan, drizzle olive oil over the top. Cover with plastic wrap and refrigerate for 4 hours. Remove from fridge and turn upside down onto a platter. Cut into 1" slices and serve.

Zucchini Noodles and Salmon
with Lemon Garlic Cream Sauce
(Serves 2)

4 zucchini, spiralized into noodles
Salt and pepper
6 ounce salmon fillet
3 tablespoons olive oil, divided
1 cup heavy cream
4 tablespoons lemon juice
2 teaspoons minced lemon zest
1/2 teaspoon garlic powder
1/4 cup freshly grated parmesan for serving

Preheat oven to 350°. Lay zucchini noodles out on a paper towel, season well with salt. Place salmon fillet on a nonstick foil-lined baking sheet. Drizzle with 1 tablespoon of olive oil and season well with salt and pepper. Bake in oven 10-12 minutes. Remove from oven and let stand.

Dab zucchini noodles dry with paper towel. Heat remaining two tablespoons of olive oil in a large, nonstick sauté pan until shimmering. Add zucchini noodles, tossing in oil, seasoning with salt and pepper. Cook, tossing often, about 5-7 minutes, until zucchini begins to soften.

In a small sauce pan, bring heavy cream to boil on medium high heat. Turn down heat to low and add lemon juice, zest, and garlic powder, whisking constantly. Season with salt and pepper. Pour lemon cream sauce over zucchini noodles. Cut salmon fillet into bite-sized pieces and fold into zucchini noodles, making sure to coat all pieces with lemon cream sauce. Season once more with salt and pepper. Serve, garnished with fresh parmesan.

Zucchini Roll Ups

(Yields 9-12 roll ups)

4 zucchini, sliced lengthwise into 1/4" thick pieces
Salt and pepper
2 tablespoons olive oil, divided
8 basil leaves, chopped, plus additional leaves for roll ups and garnish
1 teaspoon minced garlic
2 14-ounce cans puréed tomatoes
1/2 6-ounce can tomato paste (3 ounces)
1 teaspoon butter
Sliced prosciutto, cut into the width of zucchini slices
Ball of fresh mozzarella, excess water dried off

Lay zucchini slices on a paper towel, season both sides with salt and pepper. Let "sweat" while preparing marinara sauce.

In a medium sauce pan, heat 1 tablespoon olive oil until hot and shimmering. Add garlic and basil, cook for 2 minutes, stirring with a wooden spoon. Add in puréed tomatoes and paste, stirring until blended. Season with 1 teaspoon of salt and 1/2 teaspoon pepper. Stir in butter and reduce heat to low. Let simmer until ready to use.

Dab zucchini slices dry with a paper towel. In a flat sauté pan, heat remaining tablespoon of olive oil to medium high heat. Cook zucchini slices 1-2 minutes per side. Remove from heat; let cool and drain on a paper towel.

Preheat oven to 400°. Assemble zucchini roll ups by laying prosciutto, mozzarella pieces, and basil leaves on the zucchini slices. Roll it up and secure it with a toothpick. Repeat with remaining zucchini slices and ingredients.

Pour marinara into 8"x8" baking dish. Lay zucchini roll ups on their side in the marinara. Bake in oven 10 minutes, remove and serve immediately, garnished with additional basil leaves.

Zucchini Noodles Alfredo

(Serves 4)

---

4 zucchini, spiralized into noodles
Salt and pepper
4 tablespoons salted butter
1 clove garlic, minced
1/2 teaspoon fresh minced oregano
1 cup heavy cream
1 cup freshly grated parmesan, plus more for garnish
1 tablespoon chopped Italian parsley, for garnish

Spiralize zucchini into noodles, setting them aside in a large bowl. Season with salt and let them "sweat" while you prepare the sauce.

Heat the butter until melted in a large, nonstick pan over medium high heat. Add the minced garlic and oregano, stir 1 minute. Add heavy cream, bring to a boil, turn heat down to medium, season with pepper, and cook about 5-7 minutes until sauce reduces, making sure to stir with a wooden spoon every 10-15 seconds so a film doesn't form on the surface. Add parmesan and stir in until mixed and melted.

Dab the zucchini noodles dry with a paper towel. Heat a separate sauté pan to medium high heat. Cook the zucchini noodles, tossing gently, about 2-3 minutes until slightly softened. Season noodles with salt and pepper. Transfer noodles into alfredo sauce and toss until noodles are covered in sauce. Serve immediately with freshly grated parmesan and chopped Italian parsley.

GREEN CURRY SWEET POTATO NOODLES WITH EGGPLANT

(Serves 4)

1 tablespoon olive oil
1/2 sweet onion, thinly sliced
1 red bell pepper, thinly sliced
1 teaspoon grated fresh ginger
3 tablespoons sugar free green curry paste
7 fresh basil leaves, chopped
1 14-ounce can full fat coconut milk/cream (check label for no sugar)
1/4 cup water
1 eggplant, sliced, sweated, then cut into 1" chunks
1 tablespoon fish sauce
1 large or 2 medium sweet potatoes, spiralized into noodles

Heat olive oil to medium high heat in a large, flat-bottomed sauté pan. Cook onion, red bell pepper, ginger, and curry paste until aromatic and soft, about 4-5 minutes. Stir in basil and sauté 2 more minutes. Pour in coconut milk, water, then add in eggplant pieces and fish sauce, bring to boil. Turn down heat to low, add in sweet potato noodles, toss gently to coat in coconut milk. Cover and simmer on low for 10-12 minutes, being careful not to overcook noodles into mush. Serve immediately.

SAVORY MASHED SWEET POTATOES

(Serves 6-8)

---

2 pounds sweet potatoes, peeled and cut into 1-2" chunks
4 tablespoons salted butter
2 tablespoons chopped fresh sage leaves
1 teaspoon minced garlic
3/4 cup whole milk
1/4 cup heavy cream
Salt and pepper

In a large pot of boiling water, boil sweet potato pieces until tender when pierced with a fork, about 10-12 minutes. Remove from water and let drain. Put potato pieces through a potato ricer or a masher until the consistency of mashed potatoes.

In a small saucepan, heat butter on medium heat until bubbling. Add sage leaves, cook for 5 minutes. Add garlic and cook for another 2 minutes, being careful not to burn. Reduce heat if needed. Whisk in milk and cream. Heat up mixture until small bubbles form, being careful not to scald. Season with salt and pepper and remove from heat. Pour onto mashed sweet potatoes and stir to combine evenly, season once more with salt and pepper. Serve immediately.

Parsnip Purée

(Serves 4)

---

2 pounds parsnips, peeled and chopped into 2" chunks
1 tablespoon olive oil
1 teaspoon fresh thyme leaves
1/2 teaspoon minced garlic
1/2 cup full fat, sugar free coconut cream/milk (or heavy cream)
1/8 teaspoon teaspoon nutmeg
Salt and pepper

In a large sauce pan, bring 6 cups of water to boil. Cook parsnip chunks for 15 minutes, until soft when pierced with a fork. Remove parsnips from water and dry them off.

In a small sauté pan, heat olive oil on medium high heat and cook thyme leaves and garlic for two minutes, until fragrant. Add in coconut cream, whisk in nutmeg and season with salt and pepper. Bring to boil for an additional two minutes, whisking constantly. Remove from heat.

In a food processor or strong blender, pulse parsnip chunks and coconut cream mixture until smooth like the consistency of mashed potatoes. Serve immediately.

Butternut Squash Fries with Spicy Ranch Dressing

(Serves 2-3)

1 butternut squash
3 tablespoons olive oil
1 tablespoon dried oregano
1 tablespoon dried thyme
1 tablespoon dried dill
1 tablespoon dried rosemary
1 teaspoon salt
1 teaspoon onion powder
1 teaspoon garlic powder

Preheat oven to 400°. Put butternut squash in microwave and cook on high for 3 minutes. Remove and let cool for 15 minutes. Cut off top and end of squash and discard. Carefully cut off the peel and discard. Cut squash in half lengthwise and scrape out and discard the seeds on the inside. Cut squash halves into long strips, about 1/2" thick and 3" long. In a small mixing bowl, whisk together olive oil, oregano, thyme, dill, rosemary, salt, onion powder, and garlic powder. In a large plastic bag, add the squash pieces and whisked spices, sealing the top of the bag. Shake vigorously until all the squash pieces are coated. Pour the pieces onto a parchment paper lined baking sheet. Cook on bottom rack of oven for 10 minutes, flip each piece over and cook another 10 minutes, until golden brown. Remove from oven and serve with Spicy Ranch Dressing.

Spicy Ranch Dressing

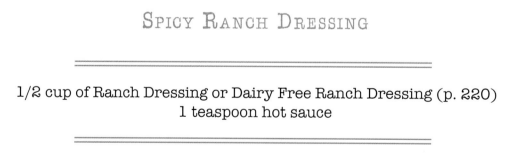

1/2 cup of Ranch Dressing or Dairy Free Ranch Dressing (p. 220)
1 teaspoon hot sauce

Whisk dressing and hot sauce into a spicy sauce. Add more hot sauce for more spice. Serve with Butternut Squash Fries.

SWEETS

Reminder About The Sweets Chapter:

Sweets are wonderful, occasional treats for the special moments in life. If you are just starting to cut out sugars and grains, please wait at least 60 days to retrain your tastebuds before making any dessert recipe with sugar in it. Sugar is sugar, and we're trying to reduce the amount we intake. But when making a very special treat, I want to make sure my audience has homemade, healthy options for desserts, made with the least amount of sugar possible to make the recipe work. Sweets are yummy! But still addictive... so be a grown up and decide for yourself just how much you can or can't handle. That said, here are some brand new delicious sweet recipes to tickle your fancy.

Mango Orange Dreamsicles

(Yields 6-8 pops)

---

2 mangoes, peeled, cored, and cut into cubes
2 oranges, peeled and deseeded
1/2 14-ounce can sugar free, full fat coconut milk/cream
1 cup water

Purée all ingredients in a Vitamix or other strong blender about 60 seconds, or until smooth. Pour into popsicle molds, freeze 4-6 hours.

Peach Pops

(Yields 6 -8 pops)

---

3 peaches, sliced
1 cup heavy cream
1/2-3/4 cup water

Reserve two peach slices per popsicle mold, and place one in each popsicle mold, setting additional slice aside. Place remaining peach slices, heavy cream, and 1/2 cup water in a Vitamix or other strong blender and purée, about 20-30 seconds. Add 1/4 cup more water and remix if the peaches and cream mixture looks too thick to pour. Pour half of peaches and cream into popsicle molds over the one peach slice in each mold. Place second peach slice into each mold and pour remaining peaches and cream mixture to fill out molds evenly. Freeze 2-4 hours, then serve.

Dark Chocolate Almond Butter Balls

(Yields 10 balls)

1/2 cup creamy almond butter
1/4 cup chopped raw almonds, plus additional 2 tablespoons for garnish
3 pitted dates, minced
2 tablespoons coconut flour
2 tablespoons ground flax meal
1/2 teaspoon vanilla or vanilla powder
1/2 teaspoon cinnamon
1/4 teaspoon salt
2 ounces 85% cacao dark chocolate, melted
1/8 cup shredded coconut flakes, for garnish

In a mixing bowl, whisk together almond butter, 1/4 cup of chopped raw almonds, dates, coconut flour, flax meal, vanilla, cinnamon, and salt until well blended and soft. Using a cookie scooper or teaspoon, form into 1-inch balls. Dip into melted dark chocolate and place on a parchment paper lined baking sheet. Sprinkle with remainder of chopped almonds and coconut flakes. Put in freezer for 30 minutes to let harden. Serve or store in fridge or freezer.

LIME TART

(serves 6-8)

CRUST

1 cup almond flour
1/2 cup coconut flour
1 stick (1/2 cup) butter, melted
1 tablespoon raw honey

Preheat oven to 350°. Combine all ingredients in a medium mixing bowl until you form a thick dough ball. Press into a 9.5" pie plate evenly and up sides. Bake for 18-20 minutes in center of oven until pie crust is light golden brown. Remove from oven and let cool.

FILLING

4 limes at room temperature (5 limes if they are small)
3/4 cup raw sugar or coconut sugar
1 stick (1/2 cup) unsalted butter at room temperature
5 large eggs at room temperature
1/4 teaspoon salt
Heavy cream, whipped for garnish
Strawberries, chopped for garnish

Remove the zest of all the limes with a zester, avoiding the white pith. Put the lime zest and the sugar in a food processor or blender and process for 1 minute, until the zest is very finely minced.

Squeeze the limes to make 1/2 cup of lime juice. In an electric mixer (or with a hand mixer), cream the butter with the sugar/lime zest mixture. Add the eggs one at a time and continue mixing. Then add the lime juice and the salt until mixed.

Pour the combined mixture into a sauce pan and cook over medium low heat, stirring constantly with a wooden spoon until thickened, about 10-12 minutes. Do not let the mixture boil. Once thickened, remove from heat and fill the tart crust with the thickened lime mixture, and allow to set at room temp for 15-20 minutes. Put tart into the fridge at least 2-4 hours, then serve with fresh whipped cream and strawberries.

APPLE PIE WITH CRUMBLE TOPPING

(Serves 6-8)

CRUST

2 tablespoons ground flax meal
4 tablespoons water
1 cup coconut flour
1/2 cup salted butter, softened to room temperature
2 tablespoons honey or coconut nectar
1/4 teaspoon salt
Coconut oil to grease the pan

Preheat oven to 400°. In a small bowl, whisk together flax meal and water. Let sit for 5 minutes. Mix together coconut flour, butter, honey, salt, until combined, but not over mixed. Pour in flax meal water, mix in, being careful not to overmix. Press into 9.5" pie pan evenly. Bake for 10-12 minutes until crust is golden. Remove from oven and let cool completely.

FILLING

10 apples, peeled, cored, and chopped into 1/2" pieces
(I use an even mix of Granny Smith and Honeycrisp)
Juice of half a lemon
1/4 cup water
2 tablespoons coconut nectar
2 tablespoons cinnamon
1/2 teaspoon allspice
1/2 teaspoon salt

Sprinkle lemon juice over apple pieces. In a large, deep sauce pan over medium high heat, heat up apple pieces in water. Cover. Turn heat down to medium and let simmer for 15 minutes. Remove from heat. Let stand for 10 minutes. Preheat oven to 400°. In a small bowl, mix together coconut nectar, cinnamon, allspice, and salt. Pour over and fold into apple pieces until they are coated. Pour apple pieces into cooled pie crust. Assemble Crumble, spread atop pie, then cook in oven 15-20 minutes until golden brown.

CRUMBLE

1/2 cup chilled salted butter, cut into cubes
1/2 cup coconut sugar
2 teaspoons cinnamon
1/2 teaspoon salt
2 tablespoons coconut flour

Combine all ingredients and using a pastry mixer or whisk, smash and mix into a crumble, being careful not to over mix and overheat the butter. Dollop bits of crumble atop the pie before baking..

Chocolate Soufflés

(Makes 4 soufflés)

I've been making a version of this soufflé since the year 2000. That's almost two entire decades of gluten free, grain free goodness. This is such an easy recipe to make, you will wonder why the heck I didn't share it with y'all earlier. My bad, lovelies. I just had to create an even lower carb version that still tastes like heaven, and that took a little extra time. This is the richest, cakiest dark chocolate soufflé you could ever ask for—these puppies sure beat the pants offa those nasty "mug cakes." I highly recommend serving with whipped cream, or the Strawberry "Ice Cream" from Eat Happy. If you can't find coconut nectar at your local grocery store, you can use honey.

1/2 cup unsalted butter, plus extra for greasing ramekins
7 ounces 85% cacao chocolate (I like Green & Black)
1/3 cup coconut nectar (or raw honey)
4 eggs, separated into four yolks and two whites
(discard two remaining egg whites)
1 cup heavy cream
1 teaspoon vanilla

Preheat oven to 350°. In a small saucepan on low heat, melt the butter and chocolate, stirring constantly. Remove from heat. In a medium mixing bowl, whisk together coconut nectar and the four egg yolks. Whisk in melted chocolate butter mixture.

In a separate mixing bowl, whisk two egg whites with a hand mixer until soft peaks form. Gently fold the beaten egg whites into the chocolate mixture until folded in evenly.

Grease 4 small ramekins with butter, place them on a foil-lined baking sheet. Pour batter evenly into the ramekins. Bake in oven 25-30 minutes, remove and let cool 5-10 minutes.

In a small metal bowl, whip the heavy cream and vanilla until stiff peaks form. Garnish chocolate soufflé with a dollop of whipped cream and serve immediately.

Red Velvet Cupcake Tops

(Yields 15-16 cupcake tops)

1/2 cup coconut or avocado oil
2 ounces dark chocolate (85% cacao or higher)
2 15-ounce cans of beets, drained
1 teaspoon vanilla
1 tablespoon ground flax meal
3 tablespoons cocoa powder
1 cup almond flour
1/3 cup coconut flour
1 teaspoon white vinegar or white wine vinegar
1/2 teaspoon baking soda
1/4 teaspoon salt
Coconut oil spray to grease the baking sheet

Preheat oven to 375°.

Melt coconut oil and dark chocolate together in a small sauce pan on medium low heat, or in a glass bowl in the microwave for 1-2 minutes, being careful not to burn. Purée the beets in a blender or Vitamix until smooth. Add the melted coconut oil and dark chocolate, vanilla extract, cocoa powder, and ground flax meal to the blender and pulse until mixed thoroughly. In a separate bowl, mix together the almond flour, coconut flour, white wine vinegar, baking soda, and salt. Then add to the blender and blend until thoroughly combined, scraping down the sides of the blender to make sure all ingredients get mixed in. Line a baking sheet with parchment paper, and spray with coconut oil. Using a 2" cookie scooper or tablespoon, scoop the batter onto the baking sheet about 3 inches apart. Bake for 30-35 minutes. Remove from oven and let cool for 5 minutes before removing tops to a wire rack or paper towel to finish cooling. If desired, put icing on tops only when completely cooled.

Icing

1/4 cup coconut sugar
1/4 cup coconut nectar
1 teaspoon vanilla
1 14-ounce can of refrigerated coconut cream (cream only, water discarded)

Blend coconut sugar, coconut nectar, vanilla, and coconut cream with a hand mixer or whisk until thoroughly blended. Refrigerate at least 30 minutes for icing to firm up. Frost the cupcake tops as desired.

Pumpkin Bars Two Ways

(Yields 9-12 bars)

Note: The cream cheese frosting version of this recipe is very rich because the frosting is very rich. You may want to add more sweet to the frosting to taste. The maple walnut glazed version is sweet on its own, so no need to tweak the sweet.

---

1 15-ounce can pumpkin purée
1/2 cup almond butter
2 eggs
3 tablespoons coconut flour
1/2 cup almond flour
1/2 cup coconut nectar (or raw honey)
1 teaspoon vanilla
2 tablespoons ground cinnamon
2 teaspoons ground ginger
1 teaspoon allspice
1/2 teaspoon ground cloves
1/4 teaspoon nutmeg
1/4 teaspoon salt
1/2 teaspoon baking soda
Coconut oil spray to grease an 8"x8" pan

Preheat oven to 350°. In a large mixing bowl, combine all ingredients until mixed into a batter. Pour into 8"x8" baking dish greased with coconut oil spray. If using Maple Walnut Glaze, bake 35 minutes, remove dish from oven, evenly pour on Maple Walnut Glaze mixture, put back in oven and bake for 10 more minutes. Remove from oven and let cool to room temperature. Cut and serve.

If using Cream Cheese Frosting, bake for 45 minutes, remove from oven and let cool to room temperature. Frost with Cream Cheese Frosting. Cut into bars and serve.

CREAM CHEESE FROSTING (DAIRY FULL)

8 ounces cream cheese at room temperature
2 tablespoons coconut nectar
1 tablespoon whole milk
1 teaspoon vanilla

Whisk together all ingredients with a hand mixer or whisk until blended into a creamy frosting. Spread onto pumpkin bar pan after it's cooled fully.

MAPLE WALNUT GLAZE (DAIRY FREE)

1 teaspoon coconut oil, melted
2 tablespoons maple syrup
1 teaspoon vanilla
Salt for seasoning
1 cup walnut pieces (or you can use pecan pieces)

In a small mixing bowl, whisk together coconut oil, maple syrup, and vanilla, then season lightly with salt. Add in walnut pieces, stirring to coat them with sugar mixture. Pour evenly over pumpkin bars after 35 minutes in oven, then put back in oven for 10 more minutes.

Pumpkin Seed Brittle

(Serves 8-10)

Note: You can find coconut nectar in the alternative sugars section of the baking aisle. It has a much milder sweet taste than honey or regular sugar. You can also use honey if you don't have access to coconut nectar. Also note, this recipe requires that the pumpkin seeds completely cool before you peel them off and break them into pieces.

---

1 tablespoon ground cinnamon
1/2 teaspoon sea salt
1/4 teaspoon nutmeg
1/4 teaspoon ground ginger
1/8 teaspoon ground cloves
1 6-ounce bag pumpkin seeds
3 tablespoons coconut nectar (or you can use honey)

Preheat oven to 350°. Line a baking sheet with nonstick foil.

In a small bowl, whisk the cinnamon, salt, nutmeg, ginger, and cloves together. In a medium bowl, fold pumpkin seeds and coconut nectar until seeds are coated. Pour spices over pumpkin seeds, stirring gently to distribute spices evenly onto the coconut nectar coating.

Spread coated pumpkin seeds onto foil-lined baking sheet, bake 15 minutes. Remove from oven and let cool completely. Peel the foil lining from the cooled pumpkin seeds and break into brittle-like pieces. Enjoy or keep stored in an airtight container for up to 7 days.

GRAIN FREE DAIRY FREE CHOCOLATE CHIP COOKIES

(Yields 12-15 cookies)

1/4 cup coconut or red palm shortening (or use coconut oil)
1/4 cup almond butter
1/2 cup coconut sugar
2 tablespoons coconut nectar
1/2 teaspoon vanilla
1/4 teaspoon salt
2 eggs
3/4 cup coconut flour, firmly packed
1/2 cup chopped 85% cacao chocolate
Coconut oil spray for baking sheet

Preheat oven to 325°. In a large mixing bowl, whisk together shortening, almond butter, coconut sugar, coconut nectar, vanilla, and salt. Beat in eggs one at a time. Fold in coconut flour, 1/4 cup at a time, mixing in thoroughly. Fold in chopped chocolate pieces.

Spray a baking sheet with coconut oil. Using your hands, make 2" balls with the dough, then place on baking sheet and press down into a circle about 1/2" thick. Bake in oven 10-11 minutes, or until cooked through. Remove baking sheet from oven and let cool, then remove cookies from baking sheet and keep stored in an airtight container for up to 5 days. Just kidding. I know you're gonna eat all of them as soon as you bake them.

COOKIE CUTTER COOKIES

(Yields 2 dozen cookies)

Sugar Cookies are a holiday tradition in my family for generations. I still have my mother's and grandmother's cookie cutters, and I love getting them out every year to make Christmas cookies for my family. But the sugar content in my old gluten free sugar cookie recipe is through the roof! I just can't do it anymore.

These Cookie Cutter Cookies are grain free and very low sugar in both the cookie and the icing components. I always strive to make my sweet treats with the least amount of sugar possible to make a recipe work.

Since these cookies don't have any type of grain/flour to hold them together, make sure you handle them gently throughout the baking process.

Oh, and when you prepare the icing, use this trick: keep your cans of coconut cream/coconut milk in the fridge over night, open the can, punch a knife through the cream and drain the water off, and you'll be left with just the creamiest part to use as the base for your icing.

Cookies

2 cups finely ground almond flour
1/4 teaspoon salt
1/4 teaspoon baking soda
1 tablespoon coconut sugar
1/2 stick (4 tablespoons) butter, melted
1/4 cup coconut nectar (or honey)
1 teaspoon vanilla extract

In a large mixing bowl, whisk together almond flour, salt, baking soda, and coconut sugar. In small mixing bowl, whisk together melted butter, coconut nectar, and vanilla extract. Add the wet ingredients to the dry ingredients, using a wooden spoon to combine into a dough, making sure to mix well. Remove dough from bowl and wrap in plastic wrap or parchment paper. Place in fridge for 1-2 hours.

Preheat oven to 350°. Between two pieces of parchment paper, roll out dough with a rolling pin to 1/4" thickness. Cut out shapes with cookie cutters, very gently place cookies onto nonstick baking sheet. Bake for 10-13 minutes, checking to make sure they don't burn. Remove from oven, and very gently lift cookies from baking sheet using a flat spatula onto paper towels to cool completely before frosting.

Dairy Free Frosting

Yields 1 cup frosting

1 cup coconut cream, chilled (all excess water drained, see note above)
2 tablespoons coconut nectar
1 teaspoon lemon juice
1/2 teaspoon vanilla
Food coloring (optional for decorating cookies)

In medium mixing bowl, whisk together all frosting ingredients until smooth and creamy. Add in food coloring if desired, then spread frosting atop cookies and serve immediately or refrigerate until serving.

Lemon Poppyseed Mini Muffins

(Yields 18 mini muffins or 6-8 large muffins)

These little muffins are the perfect bite-sized treat. I rarely make the lemon glaze topping because I think the muffin on its own is sweet enough. However, I included the glaze recipe in case you are making a treat for someone who hasn't given up sugar yet who might wonder why one would call a muffin a "sweet treat." These little bit sized lemony morsels will for sure please everyone.

Muffin Batter

Coconut oil spray for muffin tin
1¼ cups almond flour
1/4 cup coconut flour
1/2 teaspoon baking soda
1/2 teaspoon salt
2 eggs
2 tablespoons honey or coconut nectar
2 tablespoons almond milk
2 tablespoons lemon juice
1 teaspoon lemon zest, finely minced
2 tablespoons coconut oil, melted
1 tablespoon poppy seeds

Preheat oven to 350°. Spray mini muffin tin with a coating of coconut oil spray.

In a large mixing bowl, whisk together almond flour, coconut flour, baking soda, and salt. In a smaller mixing bowl, combine eggs, honey, almond milk, lemon juice, and lemon zest. Whisk wet ingredients into dry ingredients and mix thoroughly. Drizzle in melted coconut oil and mix again. Fold in poppy seeds evenly.

Using a 2" cookie scooper or tablespoon, spoon batter evenly into mini muffin tin cups, patting down each muffin level with the top rim of the muffin tin and bake 15 minutes, or until edges become golden brown. Remove from oven, pop muffins out of tins, let cool 5-10 minutes, and drizzle with glaze (optional).

Lemon Glaze (optional)

1/4 cup coconut oil, melted
2 tablespoons coconut nectar
2 tablespoons lemon juice

In a small nonstick sauté pan on medium high heat, heat all ingredients until warm. Drizzle over cooled lemon poppy seed muffins.

Vanilla Almond Custard Cake

(Serves 6-8)

Frosting

1 cup heavy cream
1/2 cup coconut nectar (or you can use honey or coconut sugar)
6 egg yolks
2½ tablespoons arrowroot powder
1 teaspoon vanilla extract
2/3 cup butter, softened to room temperature

Cake

Coconut spray for cake pans
6 egg whites
1 cup coconut sugar, ground in food processor to be extra fine
1 cup almond flour
2 tablespoons arrowroot powder

In a sauce pan, heat up heavy cream and coconut nectar on medium heat until slightly starting to boil. Remove from heat. In a large mixing bowl, whisk arrowroot powder and vanilla extract into egg yolks. Whisk heated cream mixture into egg yolk mixture very slowly, stirring constantly, being careful not to cook the egg yolks. Pour mixture back into saucepan on medium heat and cook, whisking constantly, until a custard forms, about 5-7 minutes. Pour into a bowl, cover with plastic wrap, and put in fridge to cool for 30-45 minutes. Remove butter from fridge to bring to room temperature.

Meanwhile, bake cake layers. Preheat oven to 350°. Spray two 8" cake pans with coconut spray. Using a hand mixer, beat egg whites until stiff peaks form. Add in 1/2 cup of the coconut sugar, continue whisking to combine, one additional minute. Fold in almond flour, remaining coconut sugar, and arrowroot powder until well mixed. Pour evenly into cake pans and bake 15-20 minutes until a toothpick inserted comes out clean. Remove from oven and let cool completely.

To finish frosting, in a small bowl, using a hand mixer, beat the room temperature butter until fluffy and then mix into the cooled custard from the fridge to form a frosting. Frost both cooled cake layers and refrigerate until ready to serve.

BREAKFAST

Bacon and Onion Quiche

(Serves 12)

Crust

1¼ cups almond flour
1 cup coconut flour
6 eggs
1/2 cup grated parmesan
1 cup butter, cut into cubes, plus more for greasing pan
1 teaspoon salt
1/8 teaspoon cayenne pepper

Preheat oven to 400°. Mix all crust ingredients in a food processor or mixer until the texture of a loose crumble. Pat this mixture evenly into the bottom and up the sides of a 10"x13" baking pan, greased with butter. Pierce the crust with a fork all over, then bake 20-25 minutes, until the crust is a light golden color. Remove from heat and let cool.

FILLING

5-6 pieces bacon
1 cup chopped sweet, yellow, or brown onion
1¼ cups grated Gruyère cheese
3/4 cup grated parmesan
2 cups heavy cream
1 cup whole milk
8 eggs
1 tablespoon salt
3/4 teaspoon fresh pepper

Preheat oven to 400°. Cook bacon in a large sauté pan on medium high heat until crispy, about 5-7 minutes. Chop into pieces, set aside on a paper towel to drain, reserving bacon grease in pan.

Reheat bacon grease over medium high heat. Add the chopped onions and cook until translucent, about 5-7 minutes. Remove from heat. Distribute the onion, bacon, Gruyère, and parmesan evenly over baked crust. In a large mixing bowl or mixer, whisk heavy cream, milk, eggs, salt, and pepper until very well blended. Pour the mixture into crust over the top of the onion, bacon, and cheese. Bake the quiche until firm, about 35-45 minutes. Cool for 15 minutes before serving, or serve at room temperature.

Bagel Rounds

(Yields 6 bagel rounds)

1½ cups shredded Colby Jack cheese
3 tablespoons cream cheese, softened to room temperature
2/3 cup almond flour
1 teaspoon sesame seeds
1/2 teaspoon garlic powder
1/2 teaspoon onion powder
1/4 teaspoon salt
1/4 teaspoon poppy seeds
1 egg
Coconut oil spray
Cream cheese, smoked salmon, dill, and capers for serving

Preheat oven to 400°. In a large mixing bowl, add shredded Colby Jack cheese, cream cheese, almond flour, sesame seeds, garlic powder, onion powder, salt, poppy seeds, and egg. Mix until well blended. Make a 2" round ball of dough, place onto a baking sheet lined with nonstick foil and sprayed with coconut oil. Press the dough ball into a 3" round circle. Repeat until you've used remaining dough. Cook in oven 10 minutes, carefully flip the bagel rounds, cook 5 more minutes. Remove from oven and serve bagel rounds topped with cream cheese, smoked salmon, dill, and capers.

JALAPEÑO, LEEK, AND WHITE CHEDDAR SCRAMBLE

(Serves 2)

4 eggs
1 tablespoon heavy cream
Salt and pepper
1 tablespoon olive oil
1 leek, white and palest green parts only, chopped
1 teaspoon minced jalapeño pepper, plus extra slices for garnish
1/4 cup freshly grated white cheddar
Red salsa, for garnish (make sure you read the label for no sugar)

Whisk eggs and heavy cream in a mixing bowl, season with salt and pepper. Heat olive oil in a nonstick sauté pan to medium heat, add leeks and minced jalapeño and sauté for 3-4 minutes, being careful not to burn the leeks. Add in the egg mixture, and fold with a spatula until cooked to your desired firmness. Sprinkle in cheddar cheese, folding eggs one more time to melt cheese. Serve immediately, garnished with additional jalapeño slices and a dollop of red salsa.

Poached Eggs with Wilted Watercress and Cherry Tomatoes

(Serves 4)

2 cups cherry tomatoes
4 tablespoons olive oil, divided
Salt and pepper
2 bunches of watercress, rough stems cut off and discarded
1/2 tablespoon balsamic vinegar
1/2 tablespoon lemon juice
1/2 teaspoon onion powder
1/2 teaspoon garlic powder
1 tablespoon white vinegar
8 eggs

Preheat oven to 400°. Place clean cherry tomatoes on a foil-lined baking sheet. Drizzle with 1 tablespoon olive oil, season generously with salt and pepper. Roast in oven 15 minutes, stir tomatoes around and continue roasting 5 more minutes. Remove from oven and let cool while making the other components.

In a large flat-bottomed pan, heat 1 tablespoon olive oil to medium high heat. Cook watercress until wilted, about 3-4 minutes, season with salt and pepper, then remove from heat. In a small mixing bowl, combine remaining 2 tablespoons olive oil, balsamic vinegar, lemon juice, onion powder, and garlic powder. Whisk in salt and pepper. Drizzle over greens.

In a large sauce pan, bring 2 quarts of water and white vinegar to a rolling boil. Poach eggs, two at a time in the boiling water by cracking open each egg and gently letting the insides of each plop into the water. Let boil for 3 minutes for a medium poached egg.

Prepare a small plate with a serving of watercress, some roasted cherry tomatoes, then remove the eggs from the water when ready with a slotted spoon and place atop the greens. Season eggs with salt and pepper. Repeat by poaching additional eggs for each portion, and serve.

Egg-plant Brunch Casserole

(Serves 6-8)

---

1 eggplant sliced into 1" slices
Salt and pepper
2 tablespoons olive oil
1 leek, white and palest green part quartered and chopped
1 teaspoon minced garlic
2 14-ounce cans diced tomatoes (check label for no sugar)
1 cup grated fresh mozzarella
6-8 eggs
1 teaspoon minced basil leaves

Place eggplant slices on baking sheet, season with salt. Let sit on counter to sweat for 30 minutes. Dab dry with paper towels. Preheat oven to 400°.

Bake eggplant slices for 10 minutes. Remove from oven.

In a large saucepan, heat olive oil to medium high heat, sauté leeks for 4-5 minutes, being careful not to burn, add garlic and cook for 2 more minutes. Add cans of tomatoes. Season with salt and pepper.

In a 9"x12" or 10"x13" baking dish, pour 3/4 of the tomato sauce. Lay eggplant slices in tomato sauce. Using two fingers, make an indentation in center of each eggplant slice. Sprinkle cheese around perimeter of eggplant slices, reserving 2 tablespoons of the cheese. Crack eggs into center of each eggplant slice. Cook in oven 12 minutes, remove from oven, add remainder of the tomato sauce and sprinkle remaining cheese, cook three more minutes or until eggs are to desired doneness and cheese is melted. Garnish with fresh basil and serve immediately.

Sweet Potato Hash with Poached Eggs

(Serves 2-3, but you can add more eggs for more people)

2 tablespoons olive oil
4 green onions, white and palest green parts chopped
1/2 cup chopped green or red bell pepper
1/2 teaspoon salt
1/4 teaspoon fresh ground pepper
1/2 teaspoon garlic powder
1/2 teaspoon onion powder
2 sweet potatoes, peeled and cubed into 1/2" pieces
5-6 eggs
3/4 cup Colby Jack shredded cheese

Heat olive oil in a large, flat-bottomed sauté pan to medium high heat. Add green onions, bell pepper, salt, pepper, garlic powder, and onion powder, and cook until soft, about 3-4 minutes. Add sweet potato pieces, tossing with vegetables. Cover and reduce heat to medium low and let potatoes cook 15-20 minutes. Gently stir once or twice without breaking potato pieces. Remove lid and make little pockets/nests in the potatoes to match the number of eggs you are poaching. Turn heat back up to medium high and gently crack an egg into each potato pocket. Let eggs cook 3 minutes for a soft-poached yolk and 4 minutes for a harder yolk. Season once more with salt and pepper and top with Colby Jack cheese. Let cheese melt and serve immediately.

SCOTCH EGGS

(Yields 6 scotch eggs)

7 eggs, divided
1 cup almond flour
1/2 teaspoon salt
1 teaspoon finely chopped parsley leaves
1 pound uncooked breakfast sausage, not in casing
1/2 cup olive oil, coconut oil, or beef tallow

Bring water to boil in a medium saucepan. Boil 6 eggs 4-5 minutes. Remove eggs from boiling water and place in an ice bath for 10-15 minutes and let cool. Gently peel eggs and set aside. Beat remaining egg in a small bowl. Whisk almond flour, salt, and parsley in a small bowl. Make a 4-6" diameter 1/4" thin breakfast sausage patty in your hand or between two pieces of parchment paper, then wrap evenly around egg, sealing off the edges so no egg is exposed. Dip into raw egg wash and then immediately into almond flour to coat. Repeat with remaining 5 boiled eggs.

In a large, flat-bottomed sauté pan, bring 1/2 cup olive oil to medium high heat. Do the sizzle test by sprinkling a small amount of almond flour into the oil. If it sizzles, it's hot enough to start frying the eggs. Fry the eggs until the sausage is cooked through, turning every few minutes, making sure almond flour does not burn. The almond flour coating is delicate, so be gentle when turning the egg to keep the coating in tact. If you have a screen or cover for the pan, keep the pan covered unless turning the eggs. Serve immediately.

EGG-LESS BENNY

(Serves 2)

1 tablespoon olive oil
2 large portobello mushrooms, sliced into 1/2" slices
1 beefsteak or heirloom tomato, sliced into 1/2" slices
1/4 teaspoon garlic powder
Salt and pepper
2 cups fresh baby spinach leaves
Hollandaise or Vegan Hollandaise, for serving
1 tablespoon capers, for garnish

Heat olive oil in nonstick sauté pan to medium high heat until shimmering. Add mushrooms and fry both sides of slices until brown, approximately 7-8 minutes per side. While mushrooms cook, season tomato slices evenly with garlic powder, salt, and pepper. Divide and arrange baby spinach on serving plates, add tomato slices on top of spinach, then place cooked mushroom slices on the tomatoes. Pour Hollandaise or Vegan Hollandaise on top, garnish with capers and serve immediately.

Hollandaise

===

4 egg yolks
1 tablespoon lemon juice
1/4 cup melted butter
1/4 teaspoon salt
1/8 teaspoon pepper
1/8 teaspoon ground cayenne

===

In a small metal mixing bowl, whisk egg yolks and lemon juice until smooth. In a small sauce pan, bring 2 inches of water to a slow boil on medium heat. Place small metal bowl with egg yolk-lemon juice mixture on top of the sauce pan and whisk constantly. Slowly pour in melted butter, still whisking. Continue constant whisking until sauce starts to thicken, about 5-7 minutes. Remove from heat, whisk in salt, pepper, and cayenne. If your sauce gets too thick, you can add in a teaspoon of warm water.

Vegan Hollandaise

===

1 cup Dairy Free Ranch Dressing (p. 220)
1-2 tablespoons lemon juice
1 teaspoon apple cider vinegar
1/4 cup water

===

Put Dairy Free Ranch Dressing (p. 220) in small sauce pan on medium low heat and add lemon juice, apple cider vinegar, and water. Warm-up sauce, stirring often, and add water, a teaspoon at a time, if hollandaise thickens too much.

Loren's Anthony Bourd' Eggs

(Serves 2)

The hubs Loren and I cook a fair amount together. He's a delightful cooking companion, great husband, and fantastic baby daddy. After 20 years of marriage, we now make fun of each other and our marriage onstage in a dual act, which for me, is a sign of a strong relationship.

One day I came home from running errands and found out we lost one of my heroes, Anthony Bourdain. This was incredibly sad news. Anthony Bourdain had an incredible impact on me, he did everything on his terms, and he will be missed. In honor of him, Loren has adapted one of his egg recipes, and it is delicious. Secret to a lasting marriage: laughter. And making each other this egg dish.

---

2 ounces hard salami slices, cut into 1/2" wide pieces
1 teaspoon butter
1 green Hatch chili pepper, seeds removed and discarded, chopped
4 eggs
Salt and pepper
2 tablespoons shredded Colby Jack cheese
2 teaspoons sour cream or crème fraîche

Heat a small nonstick pan to medium high heat and sauté salami slices until crispy, about 3-4 minutes. Remove salami to a paper towel lined plate. Melt butter in pan until bubbly, then sauté Hatch pepper until starting to soften, about two minutes. In a small mixing bowl, lightly whisk eggs, then season with salt and pepper. Pour beaten eggs over Hatch pepper and scramble to desired doneness, about 1-3 minutes. Fold in cheese until starting to melt. Fold in sour cream. Divide onto two plates and top with crispy salami slices. Serve.

Breakfast 211

Homemade Sausage, Part Two: Breakfast Sausage

(Yields 8-9 2" patties)

2 tablespoons minced fresh sage
1 teaspoon fresh thyme leaves
2 teaspoons salt
1/2 teaspoon paprika
1/2 teaspoon onion powder
1/2 teaspoon garlic powder
1/4 teaspoon fresh ground pepper
1/4 teaspoon ground cloves
1/8 teaspoon red pepper flakes
1 pound ground pork, highest fat content available
1 tablespoon olive oil, back fat, or beef tallow for frying

Whisk together all herbs and spices in a small mixing bowl. Fold into ground pork and mix evenly. Heat olive oil, back fat, or beef tallow in a nonstick pan to medium high heat. Form pork into patties and cook thoroughly, about 4-5 minutes per side. Serve immediately or store in airtight container in fridge for up to 3 days to use in recipes that call for sausage.

Paleo Banana Pancakes

(Yields 2 pancakes)

1 overripe banana
2 tablespoons coconut flour
1 egg
1 teaspoon vanilla
1 teaspoon baking soda
1/2 teaspoon cinnamon
1 tablespoon coconut oil, for frying (or you can use butter)

In a medium mixing bowl, smash banana with a fork until mushy. Add in coconut flour, egg, vanilla, baking soda, and cinnamon, mixing well. The dough will be thick. In a large, flat, nonstick sauté pan, heat coconut oil on medium high heat. Divide dough into two portions, placing each one in the pan, then using your fingers to flatten out the dough into a pancake shape. Cook for 2-3 minutes on one side, then flip and cook an additional minute on the other side. Remove from heat and serve.

BLUEBERRY MUFFINS

(Yields 6 muffins)

1/3 cup frozen wild blueberries, thawed
1½ cups almond flour
1/2 teaspoon baking soda
1/2 teaspoon cinnamon
1/2 teaspoon salt
2 eggs
2 tablespoons coconut nectar or honey (optional)
1 teaspoon vanilla
2 tablespoons almond milk
1/2 teaspoon apple cider vinegar
Spray coconut oil to grease the muffin pan

Preheat oven to 350°. Rinse blueberries, let drain in a colander while you prepare the muffin batter.

In a large mixing bowl, whisk together almond flour, baking soda, cinnamon, and salt. Add eggs, coconut nectar, vanilla, almond milk, and apple cider vinegar and gently mix with a fork until a thick batter forms. Gently fold in blueberries. Grease muffin pan with coconut spray and spoon in batter, evenly filling each cup. Bake muffins for 20 minutes, remove from oven and let cool 10-15 minutes then serve.

Bright Green Smoothie

(Serves 2)

1/2 cup ice
1/2 avocado, peeled and pitted
1/2 cup plain almond or coconut yogurt
1 cup torn romaine lettuce leaves
1 cup baby spinach leaves
1 entire sprig of mint
Juice of 1 lemon
1 cup unsweetened almond or coconut milk
1 cup water

Place ingredients in order listed above into a Vitamix, Nurtibullet, or other similarly strong blender and blend until smooth.

SAUCES, DRESSINGS, ETC.

This is the chapter that includes sauces, dressings, garnishes, and condiments that you can add to any dish to make it yummier. You'll find some of these recipes scattered throughout the book, but they're also here in their own chapter (plus some extra recipes thrown in for good measure).

PICKLED ONION

Yields 1 cup

---

1 onion, sliced thinly and then chopped a few times into smaller pieces
1 cup red wine vinegar

Place chopped onion in a bowl of red wine vinegar. Place in fridge for 4-8 hours before using in a recipe. Keep in fridge up to 10 days. Use in Short Rib Grinders (p. 60) or use as garnish on salads, roasts, or veggies.

Hollandaise

4 egg yolks
1 tablespoon lemon juice
1/4 cup melted butter
1/4 teaspoon salt
1/8 teaspoon pepper
1/8 teaspoon ground cayenne

In a small metal mixing bowl, whisk egg yolks and lemon juice until smooth. In a small sauce pan, bring 2 inches of water to a slow boil on medium heat. Place small metal bowl with egg yolk-lemon juice mixture on top of the sauce pan and whisk constantly. Slowly pour in melted butter, still whisking. Continue constant whisking until sauce starts to thicken, about 5-7 minutes. Remove from heat, whisk in salt, pepper, and cayenne. If your sauce gets too thick, you can add in a teaspoon of warm water.

Vegan Hollandaise

1 cup Dairy Free Ranch Dressing (p. 220)
1-2 tablespoons lemon juice
1 teaspoon apple cider vinegar
1/4 cup water

Put Dairy Free Ranch Dressing in small sauce pan on medium low heat and add lemon juice, apple cider vinegar, and water. Warm up sauce, stirring often, adding water a teaspoon at a time if hollandaise thickens too much.

Ranch Dressing

(Yields 1 cup)

1 cup sour cream or crème fraîche
2 tablespoons cream cheese
2 tablespoons fresh lemon juice
1 teaspoon onion powder
1 teaspoon dried dill
1 teaspoon salt
1/2 teaspoon fresh ground pepper
1/2 teaspoon garlic powder

Whisk all ingredients together and use as a dip or salad dressing.

Dairy Free Ranch Dressing

(Yields 1 cup)

1 cup cashews
1 medium zucchini, peeled and chopped (about 1 cup)
1 tablespoon lemon juice
1 tablespoon apple cider vinegar
1½ teaspoons dried dill
1 teaspoon salt
1 teaspoon onion powder
1 teaspoon garlic powder
1/2 teaspoon fresh ground black pepper
1/2 teaspoon minced fresh chives
1/8 teaspoon ground cayenne
1/4-1/2 cup water, as needed to thin out dressing

Soak cashews in water for 2-12 hours. Drain water when ready to make dressing. In a Vitamix or similar strong blender, add soaked cashews, zucchini, lemon juice, apple cider vinegar, dill, salt, onion powder, garlic powder, black pepper, chives, ground cayenne, and 1/4 cup of water. Blend to a creamy consistency, adding more water if necessary. Cover and put dressing in the fridge for 1-4 hours before serving.

Caesar Dressing

(Yield 1/2 cup)

1/2 cup mayonnaise
2 tablespoons lemon juice
2 teaspoons anchovy paste
2 teaspoons minced garlic
1 teaspoon Dijon mustard
1/2 teaspoon salt
1/4 teaspoon freshly ground pepper
4 tablespoons freshly grated parmesan cheese

In a medium mixing bowl, whisk mayonnaise, lemon juice, anchovy paste, minced garlic, Dijon mustard, salt, and pepper until creamy. Add in the parmesan cheese and let flavors marry in fridge or serve immediately.

Dairy Free Caesar Dressing

(Yields 1 cup)

---

1 cup cashews
1 medium zucchini, peeled and chopped (about 1 cup)
1 tablespoon lemon juice
1 tablespoon apple cider vinegar
1 teaspoon anchovy paste
1 teaspoon minced garlic
1 teaspoon salt
1/2 teaspoon freshly ground pepper
1/8-1/4 cup water

Soak cashews in water for 2-12 hours. Drain water when ready to make dressing. In a Vitamix or similar strong blender, add soaked cashews, zucchini, lemon juice, apple cider vinegar, anchovy paste, minced garlic, salt, and pepper. Thin with water to desired consistency.

Cilantro Green Goddess Dressing

(Yields 1 cup)

For Green goddess dressing, it is important to chop the herbs ahead of time, so the herb leaves don't get tangled and caught on the food processor blades. Also, if you're not a fan of cilantro, use flat leaf parsley or Italian parsley instead.

1/3 cup crème fraîche, or use full fat canned coconut milk for dairy free
1 large avocado, peeled and pitted
Juice of half a lemon
1/2 teaspoon minced garlic
1 teaspoon Dijon mustard
3 tablespoons chopped fresh chives
3 tablespoons chopped cilantro leaves (or you can use Italian parsley leaves)
1 tablespoon chopped tarragon
1/2 teaspoon salt
1/2 teaspoon freshly ground pepper
1-2 tablespoons water, to adjust dressing thickness

Combine all ingredients in a food processor or strong blender. Add more or less water depending on desired consistency.

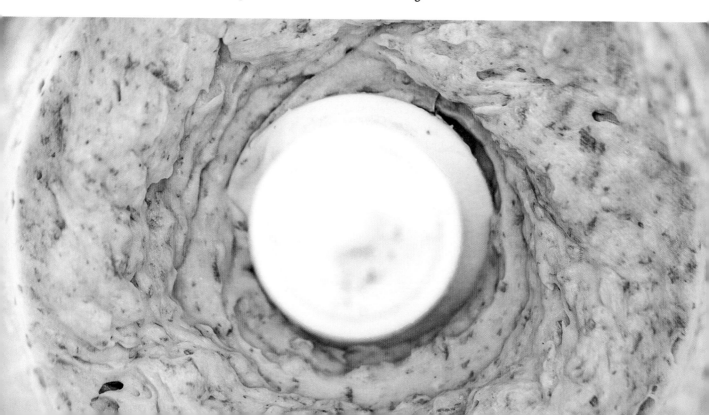

Lemon Dijon Tahini Dressing

(Yields 1 cup)

1/2 cup tahini
1/4-1/2 cup water
Juice of half a lemon
1 tablespoon Dijon mustard

Combine all ingredients in food processor. Add more or less water until you get to desired consistency.

Zhoug (Spicy Herb Pesto)

(Yields 1 cup)

Zhoug is a spicy pesto that you can make ahead to have the flavors marry beautifully over the course of a day or so. This version is a little less spicy, so if you'd like to amp up the spice, use serrano peppers, or add more fresh jalapeños, harissa, or red pepper flakes.

1 cup packed cilantro leaves
1 cup packed parsley leaves
2 fresh jalapeños, seeds and tops discarded, loosely chopped
1 4-ounce can of fire roasted green chiles, drained
2 teaspoons minced garlic
1/2 teaspoon cumin
1/2 teaspoon dried harissa
1/4 teaspoon red pepper flakes
1/4 teaspoon ground cardamom
Juice of half a lemon
1/4 cup olive oil
Salt and pepper to taste

Combine cilantro, parsley, and jalapeño in a food processor and pulse 5-10 times to tear up the leaves. Add remaining ingredients and purée until desired consistency. Add salt and pepper to taste. If you like it more spicy, add more harissa and/or red pepper flakes.

Homemade Ketchup

(Yields 2 cups)

2 teaspoons salt
1 teaspoon onion powder
1/4 teaspoon fresh ground pepper
3 tablespoons apple cider vinegar
3 tablespoons white vinegar or white wine vinegar
1 14-ounce can diced tomatoes, no sugar added
1 6-ounce can tomato paste
1/2 cup blueberries
6 Medjool dates, pitted and chopped
3/4 cup water

Combine all ingredients in a large saucepan over medium high heat. Bring to a boil, and then reduce heat, and let simmer 15-20 minutes, stirring every few minutes. Remove from heat and let cool. Pour into Vitamix or strong blender and pulse contents until completely puréed. Serve immediately, freeze, or keep in fridge for up to 10 days.

Cocktail Sauce

(Yields 1/2 cup)

1/2 cup Homemade Ketchup (see above recipe)
Juice of 1/2 lemon
1 teaspoon prepared horseradish (or more to taste)

Whisk together all ingredients for a quick homemade cocktail sauce. Serve with Torri's Hillbilly Ceviche (p. 8), Crab Cakes (p.12), or seafood dish of your choice

Remoulade Sauce

(Yields 1 cup)

1/2 cup mayonnaise
1/2 cup sour cream
1½ teaspoons Tabasco sauce or your favorite sugar free hot sauce
2 tablespoons Dijon mustard
2 tablespoons chopped chives
1 tablespoon lemon juice
1 tablespoon chopped capers
1 teaspoon minced parsley
1 teaspoon anchovy paste
1/4 teaspoon fresh ground pepper

Combine all ingredients in a small food processor. Pulse to mix, about 10-15 seconds. Serve with Crab Cakes (p. 12) or any seafood dish.

Pico De Gallo

(Yields 2 cups)

---

2 cups finely diced tomatoes, seeds removed
1/2 medium white onion, diced
3 tablespoons finely chopped cilantro
1 tablespoon finely chopped jalapeño pepper
1 tablespoon freshly squeezed lime juice
1 teaspoon salt

Combine all ingredients and stir together, being careful not to over mix. Serve with Carne Asada (p. 50), Lime Tequila Fajitas (p. 52), veggies, chicken, steak, or fish, or use as a dip.

DRINK HAPPY

I am asked on a daily basis what sort of adult beverages we can enjoy now that we've cut out sugar, and while the trusty vodka soda with lime is great, it gets boring. This chapter has a selection of classic cocktail recipes adapted to remove the use of simple syrup or sugary liqueurs and instead uses fruit for a bit of sweet. All of these recipes can be made non-acoholic as well, just omit the alcohol and use extra soda water.

Low Carb Strawberry Margarita

(Yields 1 cocktail)

Ice
2 ounces silver tequila
Juice of 1 lime (or 1 ounce)
1 ounce fresh strawberry purée (2 tablespoons)
4 ounces soda water
Squeeze of a fresh tangerine/clementine/mandarin orange (optional)
Lime wedges for garnish

Fill a margarita glass or old fashioned glass with ice. Pour in tequila, lime juice, and strawberry purée, stir. Add soda water and a squeeze of tangerine, stir again. Garnish with a lime wedge.

Mint Gimlet

(Yields 1 cocktail)

Ice
2 ounces vodka or gin
2 mint leaves, plus more for garnish
Juice of half a lime, plus lime wedges for garnish
4-6 ounces soda water, to taste

Fill a cocktail shaker with ice, pour in vodka, mint leaves, and lime juice and shake shake shake. I like my vodka ice cold, so I shake for about 20-30 seconds. The mint leaves will break up in the shaker and pour out through the strainer. Strain into an old fashioned glass filled with ice, add soda water, and garnish with mint and/or a wedge of lime.

Blueberry Thyme Gin Fizz

(Yields 1 cocktail)

1 tablespoon fresh blueberries
Juice of half a lemon
1/2 teaspoon thyme leaves, plus thyme sprigs for garnish
Ice
2 ounces gin (or vodka)
4 ounces soda water

Place blueberries, lemon juice, and thyme leaves into the bottom of an old fashioned glass and muddle for 20-30 seconds. Add ice, gin, and soda water, then stir. Garnish with fresh thyme sprig.

Drink Happy 253

Tom Collins Anisette

(Yields 1 cocktail)

You can infuse distilled alcohol with any herb, citrus, or spice of your choice. And I highly recommend you do...and that you get creative.

For this cocktail, add four to five star anise pods to 2 cups of vodka. Keep in freezer, airtight for up to a month for the anise flavor to become infused into the vodka. Strain anise pods out of vodka and discard.

---

2 ounces star anise-infused vodka
Juice of half a lemon, plus a lemon wedge for garnish
Ice
4-6 ounces soda water

Combine vodka and lemon juice in a shaker filled with ice. Shake 30 seconds, until cold. Strain out into an old fashioned glass filled with fresh ice. Top off with soda water and a lemon wedge.

The Pinkie Tuscadero

(Yields 1 cocktail)

1 tablespoon raspberries
1 tablespoon peeled, chopped cucumber
Juice of half a lime, plus lime wedges for garnish
1/4 teaspoon chopped jalapeño (no seeds), plus additional slices for garnish
2 ounces vodka, gin, tequila or rum
Soda water

In the bottom of a cocktail shaker, muddle the raspberries, cucumber, lime juice, chopped jalapeño, and vodka. Add ice and shake vigorously, at least 30 seconds. Strain into an old fashioned glass filled with ice. Top with soda water to taste, garnish with a lime wedge and a jalapeño slice.

Watermelon Mint Martini

(Yields 1 cocktail)

2 ounces vodka
1½ cups watermelon
3-4 mint leaves, plus more for garnish
Fresh limes for lime juice
Soda water (optional)

In a Vitamix or food processor, purée the watermelon with 3-4 mint leaves. Refrigerate the purée for about 30 minutes. Over ice into a cocktail shaker, squeeze 1/2 lime, 2 ounces of watermelon mint purée, and 2 ounces vodka. Shake vigorously and then strain into a martini glass. Garnish with additional mint leaves. If it tastes too sweet, you can cut it with more lime juice and/or a splash of soda water.

VODKA BELLINI

(Yields 1 cocktail)

Bellinis are usually made with Prosecco, which is quite high in sugar, so we're gonna have ours without. Make this Vodka Bellini during the summer when peaches are in season, and you won't miss the Prosecco at all.

---

2 ounces vodka, shaken ice cold
2 yellow peaches, pitted, puréed, and refrigerated cold,
plus additional peach slices for garnish
1/2 tablespoon lemon juice
4-6 ounces cold soda water
Fresh raspberries for garnish

Pour vodka, 3 tablespoons of peach purée, and lemon juice in a champagne flute or white wine glass. Top with soda water and garnish with a raspberry and a peach slice.

Cucumber Mint Mojito

(Yields 1 cocktail)

This refreshing cocktail usually has a metric ton of sugar, but this version removes the sugar and keeps it refreshing. Poblano pepper adds a warmth to it, but if you want to go spicier, try mincing jalapeño.

---

3 cucumber slices, chopped
3 raspberries
3 mint leaves, plus more for garnish
1-inch piece poblano pepper, chopped
1 ounce lemon juice
2 ounces rum
4-6 ounces soda water
Ice

In a Collins glass or double old fashioned glass, muddle cucumber, raspberries, mint leaves, and poblano pepper in lemon juice. Add rum, soda water, and ice, and serve garnished with mint sprigs.

NEW FASHIONED OLD FASHIONED

(Yields 1 cocktail)

A traditional old fashioned uses a whole sugar cube and a sugar soaked Marischino cherry, which will be far too sweet once you've forsaken sugar. This version removes the sweet which allows you to taste the flavors in the bourbon or rye.

Ice
Orange wedge
2 ounces bourbon or rye
Dash of Angostura bitters
One fresh cherry, halved and pitted, plus one with a stem for garnish
2-4 ounces Orange flavored soda water (LaCroix, Dasani, or any other brand soda water with no added sugar)

In an old fashioned glass filled with ice, squeeze the orange wedge into the glass, then twist the orange wedge to release the orange flavor in the zest and drop into the glass. Add bourbon, a dash of Angostura bitters, cherry halves, and orange flavored soda water to taste, stir and serve garnished with one more cherry.

Eat Happy Too Recipe Index

Eat Happy Too Ingredient Index